Better Homes and Gardens

Tailoring
Suits and Coats

BETTER HOMES AND GARDENS BOOKS
NEW YORK DES MOINES
Better Homes and Gardens Creative Sewing Library

Printed in the United States of America.
Third Printing.
Library of Congress Catalog Card Number: 66-8592.
SBN: 696-01203-0

CREATIVE SEWING

Beautiful fabrics and exciting pattern styles make sewing more rewarding than ever. With today's new techniques and equipment, sewing can be fun for the beginner as well as the accomplished seamstress.

Better Homes and Gardens Creative Sewing Library presents sewing methods based on common sense—practical, professional tips that show how to give clothes for the whole family a "custom-made" look.

The Creative Sewing Library has been prepared under the guidance of Miss Lucille Rivers, one of America's eminent sewing experts. To help women learn the easy, professional methods of sewing she describes in the books, she has drawn upon her long experience in the field. Miss Rivers has directed her own custom salon in New York, and she has served as consultant to many leading clothing manufacturers.

She has created new styles for fashion shows, and has lectured on sewing in department stores in this country, Australia, and New Zealand. For many years Miss Rivers was sewing editor of NBC's popular "Home Show," and she has conducted sewing demonstrations on many other television programs. In the Creative Sewing Library, she shares her fashion knowledge and dressmaking experience with you.

Titles in the Creative Sewing Library are:

Professional Sewing Tips
How to Sew for Children
Pattern Adjustments
Tailoring Suits and Coats
Sewing Casual Clothes

CONTENTS

Tailoring the dressmaker suit

This is the fashion era of the dressmaker suit. Perhaps you, like many other women, have several of these suits in your wardrobe. No matter what today's current fashion may be, somehow your favorite always seems to be in style. Each season new designs are introduced, but the styles from previous seasons are still fashionable. In fact, many of them are becoming classics. It appears that any style of the dressmaker suit is fashionable, as long as it is a flattering style on you.

Once you start doing tailoring, this type of suit may become your favorite sewing project. It offers you a feeling of accomplishment that no other type of sewing can. And, surprisingly enough, many styles of the dressmaker suit are often very easy for you to make.

Tailor's ham

When you reach the suit-making stage, you will need this tailoring and pressing aid, known as a "tailor's ham." You'll find it useful in many ways, especially for tailoring. These hams are now available in stores, but the one you make yourself will be superior in shape, size, texture—important for tailoring.

To make a ham, you'll need 3/4 yard of heavy muslin or drill. Make a pattern on heavy paper.

A. Draw a line 18 inches long (1-4), divide, mark line in thirds.

Draw a line 13 inches long across the first line, at point (2).

Draw a line 11 inches long across on the remaining line (3).

Shape of the cushion is formed by drawing from points 1-2-3-4 and back to point 1.

B. Fold on the long line, and cut around the shaping line to form the ham-shaped piece.

Mark the pattern on the drill. Allow seam allowances, and cut out, except at the wide end. Do not cut fabric off at this end.

Sew around the shape, leaving the wide end open where the fabric was not cut off. Baste the shape at this end. Baste-stitch a wide hem in the open ends of the fabric, and when you are finished, turn the shape right side out.

The ham can be stuffed with wool scraps or sawdust. Wool scraps are preferable; be sure they are colorfast. Cut up old wool blankets, wool clothes, or wool scraps. You'll need lots. Dump the wool scrap in a tub of water and let it soak.

C. Slide curtain rods through the ends of the ham, and hang it up over a sink or pan. Stuff it with wet wool scrap. Pack it down as tightly as you can, and keep putting in more scrap. Shape it as you go. When you can not get any more scrap into the ham, and you have it completely full, mold it to a finished line at the open end. Baste the two layers together along this line to hold the shaping. Hang it up to dry in a warm, dry place. Let it hang until it is completely dry—sometimes the drying takes several days.

D. When the ham is dry, trim off the excess fabric.

E. Leave the seam allowances and turn them under.

F. Sew up the open end with fine stitches, so the seam is smooth.

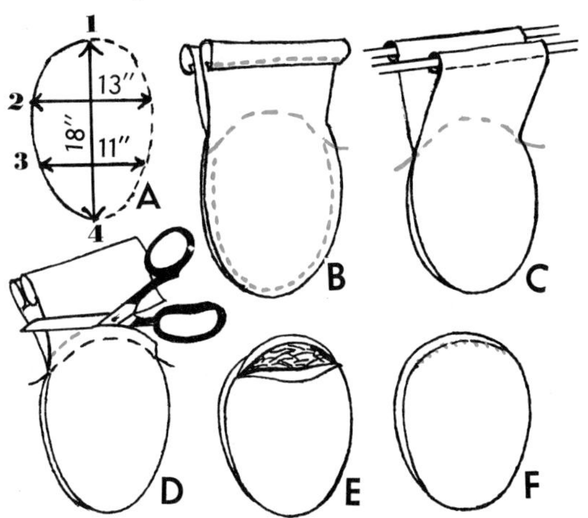

Adjustments for suit patterns

Buy your suit pattern in the same size as you do a dress pattern. Extra size is allowed in a suit for the lining and so it can be worn comfortably over a blouse.

The suit is made for the same size figure as the dress, but, because of extra ease, it will appear larger.

See the Creative Sewing Book on *Pattern Adjustments* for detailed fitting instructions. It shows how to make adjustments on a basic pattern, which almost entirely eliminates future fittings. After you have made your basic pattern, make the same adjustments in the suit pattern.

It's important that the suit fit the slope and width of the shoulders correctly, so if your basic has shoulder adjustments, be sure to make them on the suit. Sketches below show adjustments for a suit.

Adjusting shoulders

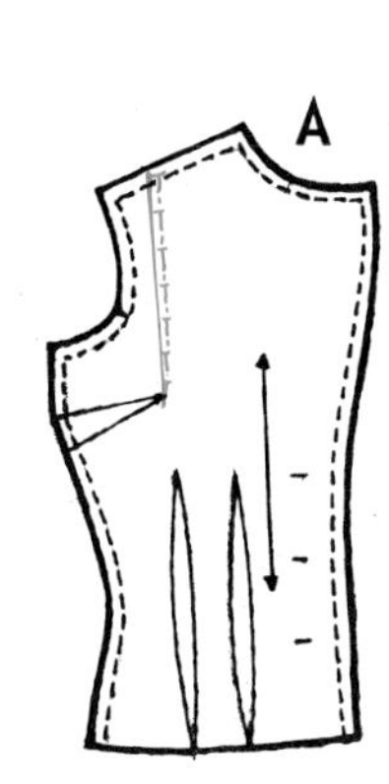

Narrow the suit shoulder with a tuck at the same point and for the same amount as on your basic pattern

(A). If the lower front of your suit jacket hangs open (B), correct it with a dart under the front neck.

Pin the dart under the neck of the suit and the facing (C). Make the dart in the same amount and at the same point as on your basic pattern, except extend it into the lapel.

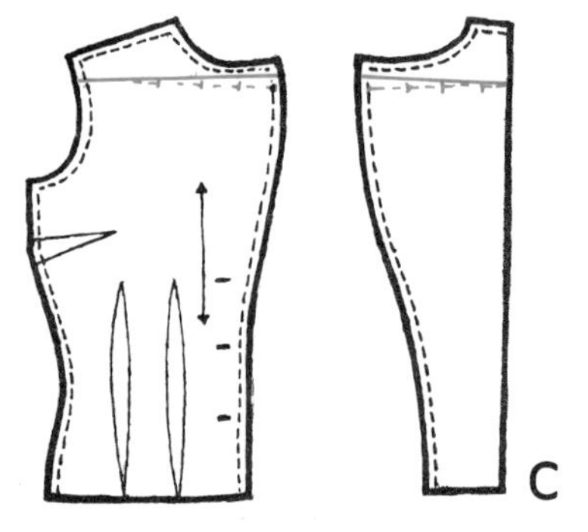

Dolman sleeve

This sleeve is confusing to many women. Because it is a loose-fitting shoulder, they believe there's no need to adjust the pattern first. Or, they are uncertain about where and how to adjust it, because there is no armhole seam. Lay basic pattern over dolman pattern. Mark where the armhole would naturally be (A).

On the dolman sleeve, pin a tuck to narrow the shoulder inside armhole mark. A dart taken under neck slopes out toward same mark (B).

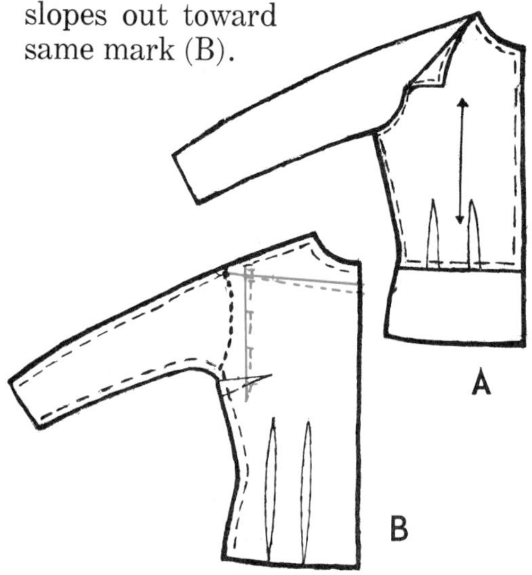

When only front shoulders have been narrowed, sew a dart in back shoulder (C). This gives a better fit, and back and front shoulder seams will be the same width.

If the necessary adjustments are not made in the shoulder of this dolman type of sleeve, the shoulder seam will twist to the back, as shown in (D).

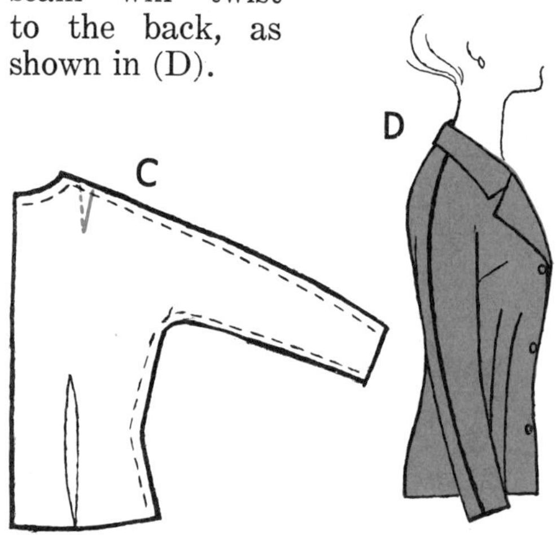

Modified dolman sleeve

In this style, there is no armhole seam at the shoulder, but the side gore forms an underarm seam. It is vital that you adjust this shoulder before cutting the suit. Because of its shaping, this sleeve cannot be corrected at a later time.

Pin side gore of muslin pattern to the front before making any adjustments. Draw a line on pattern to indicate the shoulder width (A).

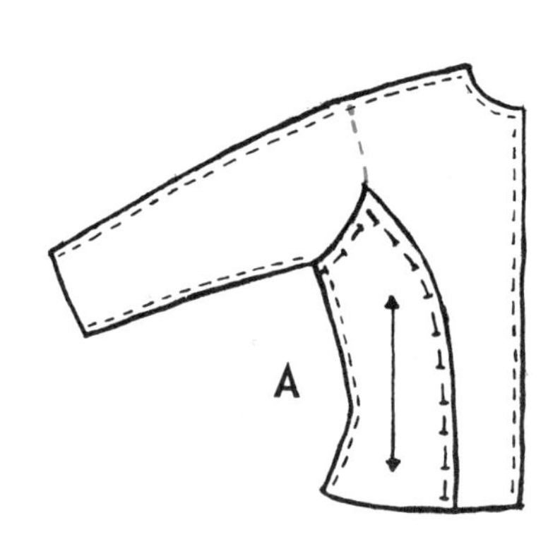

If needed, pin a dart under the neck (B). Narrow the shoulder with a tuck. Do this while the pieces are pinned together, so adjustments will be in the right place. Then unpin the pattern pieces, leaving the adjustments in place and ready to cut (C).

Make deeper back dart, or add one if there is none, for a better fit.

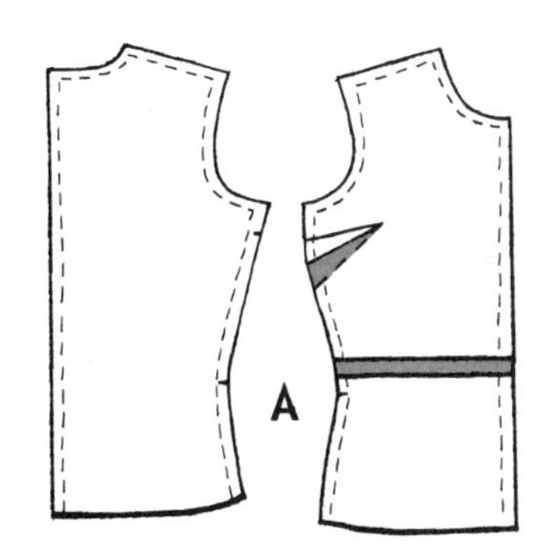

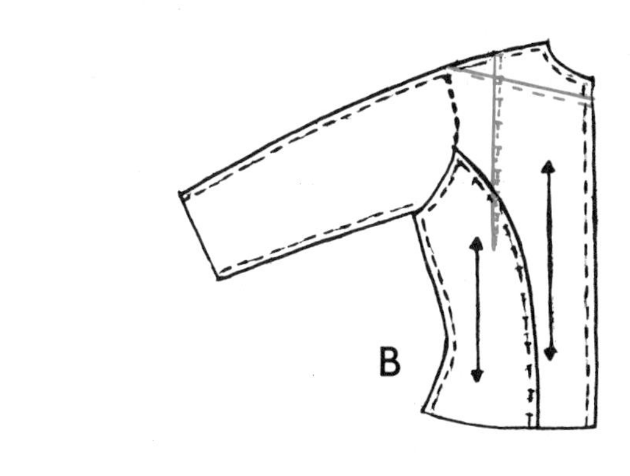

The same adjustment applies to the modified dolman sleeve.

Slash the front piece and spread the same amount you lengthened the waist on your basic pattern. Slash the side gore across through dart. The dart lines are lapped and the front edge of the gore spread. This gives greater fullness to the bust, and eliminates the dart (B).

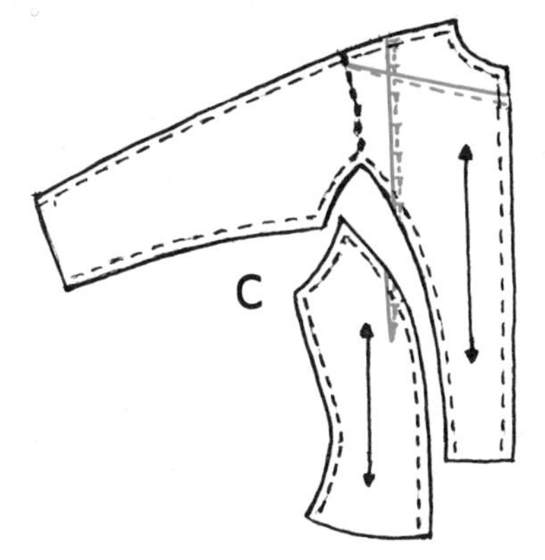

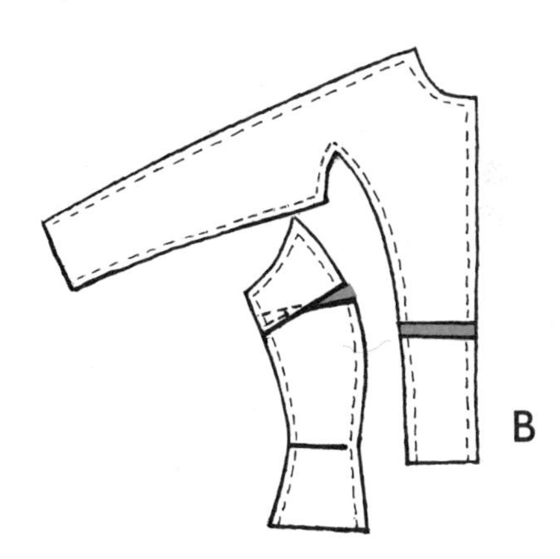

Bust adjustment

When the bust needs more fullness than the pattern allows, it is necessary to give more cupping. (See section on "Full-busted figure," in Creative Sewing Book on *Pattern Adjustments.*) Lengthen front suit pattern by same amount as on basic pattern. This extra length is taken up in the deeper dart. Deeper dart gives more cupping, and back and front side seams will be same length (A).

Same book shows how to increase for fuller bust in the princess line.

Adjusting for waistline size

If the waistline of the suit needs to be made smaller, it is easy to do some extra fitting on the front darts, and take in the side seams slightly. Fitting-in on the front darts will actually give a better fit to the bustline of the suit jacket.

The waistline can be increased by adding a small amount at the side seams (A). To increase it a larger amount, slash in on the waistline. Slash toward both the armhole and the hipline and spread apart the necessary amount (B).

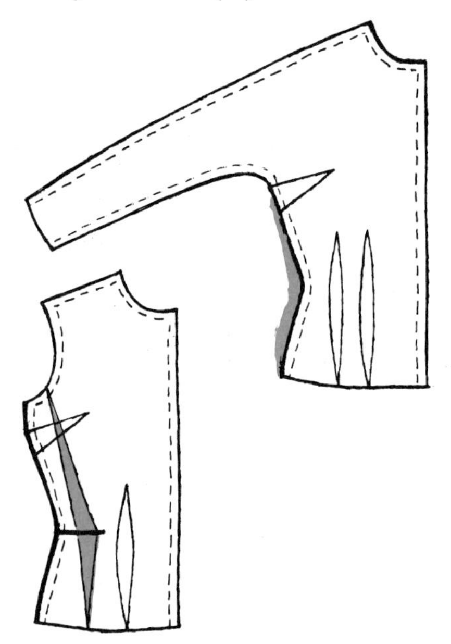

Broadening the back

Slash the pattern for the entire length to broaden the back (A).

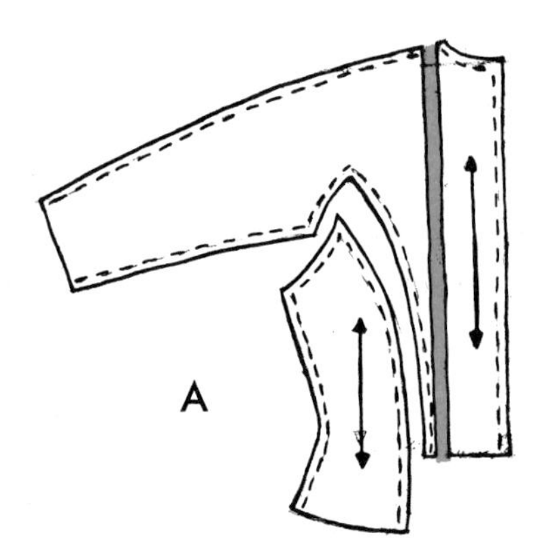

The sketches show how to broaden the shoulders only on the three types of patterns. Slash pattern under the arm and up to the shoulder. Spread the amount indicated on your basic dress muslin. At the underarm, taper seam to nothing at waist (B, C, D). When the back only has been broadened, take up the extra width in a dart at the back shoulder (C), (D).

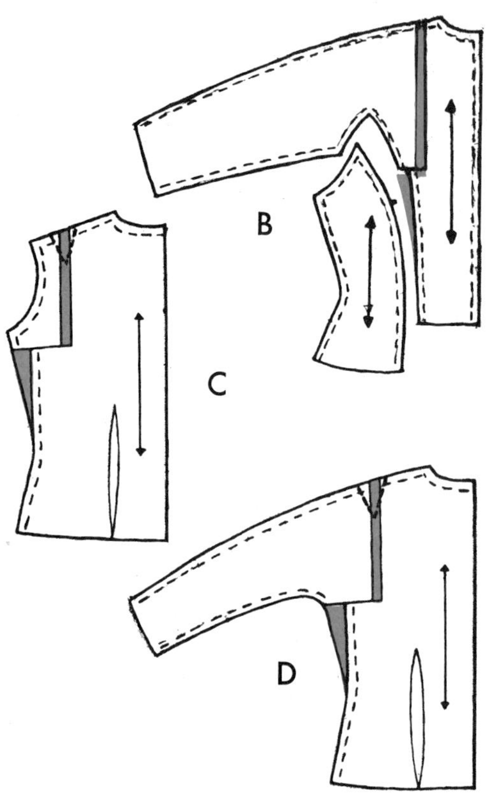

If your basic pattern needs a dart or slash under the back neckline, make the same kind of adjustment in the suit (E). Slash or fold the pattern toward the approximate armhole seam. Shorten waistline with a tuck across the pattern.

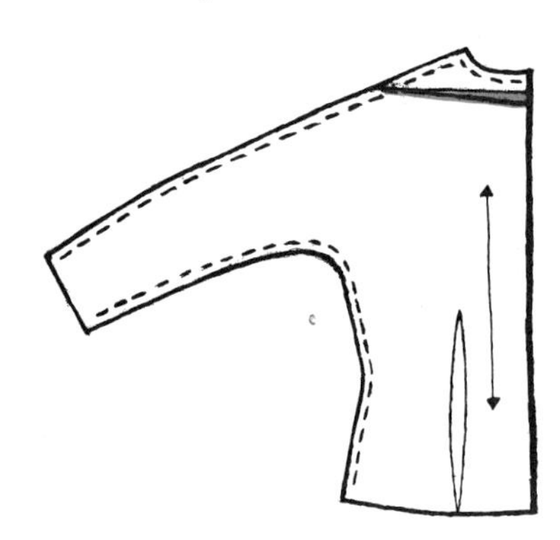

Or, lengthen by slashing at the same point on all three styles (F, G, H). Adjust according to the alteration on the basic muslin.

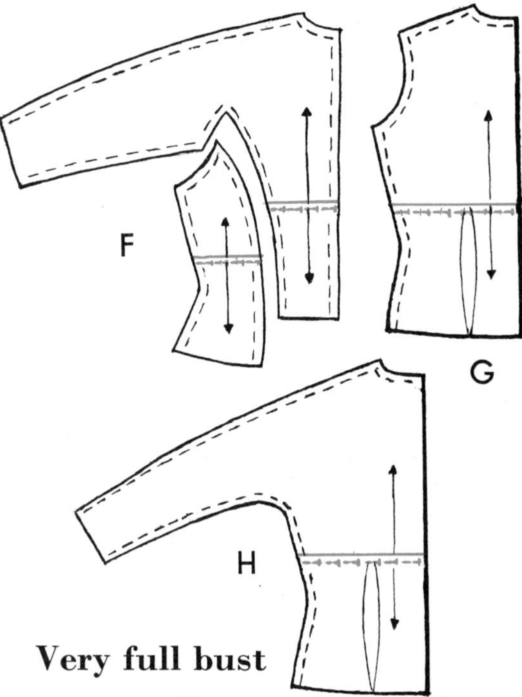

Very full bust

Since you buy a pattern according to armhole size (see Creative Sewing Book on *Pattern Adjustments*), a figure with a very large bust requires more alteration. This alteration is shown for the basic dress pattern, and must be applied to a suit in the same way. If suit has a modified dolman sleeve, or fitting is achieved with a gore, pin pieces together, forming suit front. Mark pattern where it is to be slashed; make adjustment same as in basic pattern.

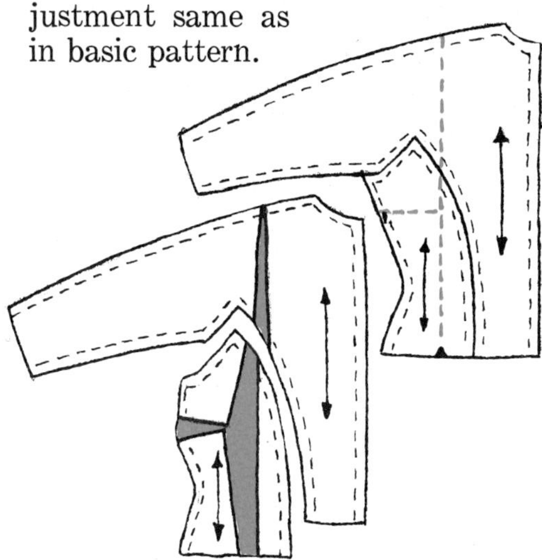

Cutting and assembling

Although dressmaker suits are made of all types of fabrics, woolens are most commonly used. Check for a nap fabric, especially on wool, since it often has surface detail that must be handled carefully.

Fleece, cashmere, broadcloth, alpaca, and camel's hair have a nap and must be cut with the nap running down. If these fabrics are cut with pieces in either direction, the finished garment will look as though it is made of two different shades.

Other fabrics, although they do not have an actual nap, may have a surface texture that will look shaded unless the pattern is cut one way.

Flannels, crepes, and most tweeds are usually safe to cut in either direction. But, it is best to cut *all* woolens one way, whenever possible. Since these fabrics are very wide, they can usually be cut one way without any waste of material.

Many suits have dolman-type sleeves. When the sleeve and body are all in one, pieces can seldom be cut in pairs from fabric on the lengthwise fold. They must be laid out on the open fabric. Lay out all the pattern pieces on the wrong side of one layer of the fabric. This is the layout for one half of the suit.

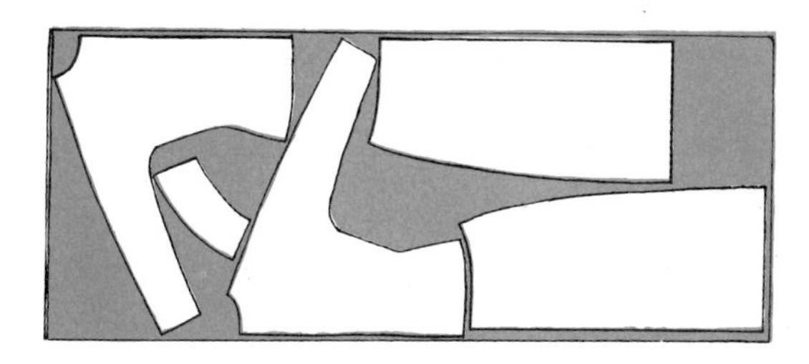

Tear or cut across the fabric.

Turn this remaining piece over so that the right side is face up. The fabric on which the pattern pieces are pinned is laid on the second length of fabric, right sides together. Be sure the nap, if any, is running in the same direction. When the suit is cut, all of the pattern pieces will be in pairs.

If you cut only one layer of fabric at a time, it is easy to make a mistake and cut two right fronts or two left backs, quite by accident.

Unpin the pattern and shake out each piece. Place the cut-out pieces together again and repin the pattern. You may find that the under piece of the fabric is slightly larger, even though both have been cut from the same pattern. This is because the surfaces of wool sometimes stick together, forming bubbles on the underside. Smooth out and recut so pieces are same size.

Next, check to see whether the wool is soft and tends to stretch. If so, it's best to mount the fabric on an underlining to give it firmness and body. Almost all fabrics should be underlined like this, except for very heavy or bulky ones.

See page 61 for information on the types of underlinings available and for instructions on how to use them.

Mark for any inside detail, such as darts or tucks, on the underlining before removing the pattern. Use tailor's chalk or a tracing wheel. Pockets, trimmings, or outside detail can be marked on the right side of the fabric with tailor's chalk and then basted, since these marks must remain on fabric for a while.

Slash at the front neck mark where the collar joins the jacket. Lay the wrong side of the jacket pieces on the unmarked side of the underlining. Then press the two pieces together and pin all around, just outside the seam allowance line. Stitch together with a large stitch on the machine. This is called "mounting the fabric." Your suit jacket will have a much firmer tex-

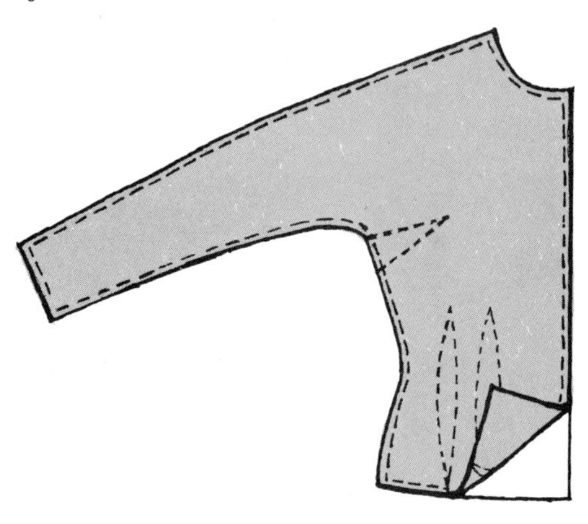

ture, be easier to handle, and stay pressed longer. Wherever there are darts, stitch the two layers of fabric together by machine through the center of dart. Then stitch darts.

When sewing darts in a suit, start from the center of the dart. Sew first to one end, then to the other, leaving about 1 inch of thread hanging. Since the suit will be lined, the threads won't show, and the dart will taper to a sharper point.

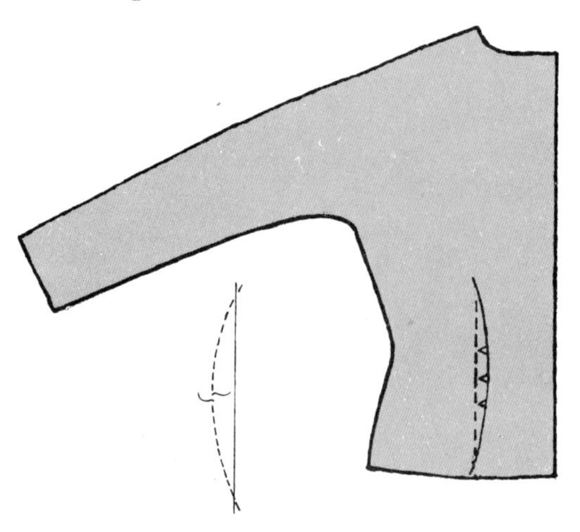

Make up any trimming details, such as pockets, bands, or bows, so they are ready to try when you fit your suit. If you plan to use braid, or other trimmings, such as a belt, contrasting collars, unusual buttons, have them all handy so you can try them and decide on final trim.

Sew the underarm and shoulder seams, but do not press them. Sew the sleeve seams so sleeves are ready to try. Don't press any part of the suit at this point. The first pressing is the most important, since this is when the molding and shaping are done. This permanently affects the fit and appearance of the suit.

Instead of pressing the seams and darts, baste them to one side so they will be flat while you are trying on the suit. Sew the easing stitches in the sleeve cap.

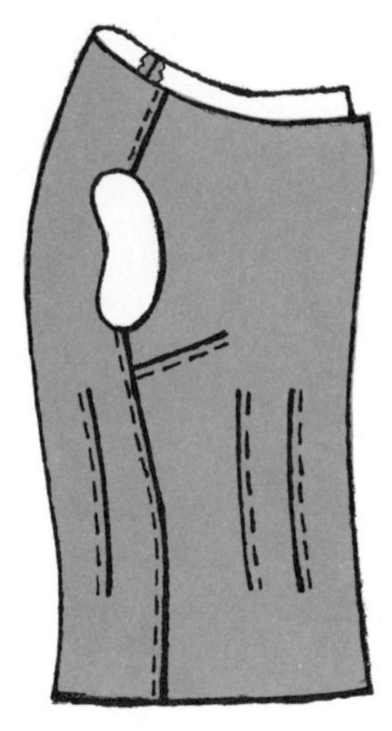

Using a large stitch, now sew two rows—one on the seam allowance line, the second 1/4 inch from the sleeve edge. Sew from underarm notch completely around the sleeve, back to underarm notch.

Baste the seams on the sleeves to one side. Press a very light crease into the suit sleeves for the fitting. On a two-piece sleeve, lay the sleeve on the ironing board with the under sleeve up. At the lower end of the sleeve the crease should be at the back seamline.

As you press, the front crease at the top of your sleeve should be 1¼ inches from the front underarm seam. Now ease in fullness around sleeve.

The top of the sleeve should be flat for about 1 inch. Fullness at the back should come on either side of the back sleeve seam, and the cap of sleeve should be eased on either side of top. Also ease in the sleeve slightly under the arm, so that it fits high and snug to the armhole. Then baste into jacket for the fitting.

If you are using a basic pattern for fitting, as shown in the Creative Sewing Book on *Pattern Adjustments,* and have adjusted the skirt according to the basic, your suit skirt can be sewed and pressed before the fitting. (This same book also shows all the fitting points to check, and tells you how to adjust both the jacket and the skirt. By following this fitting method, any adjustments needed later, will be minor ones.)

Make up the waistband for your skirt, and baste it to the waistline.

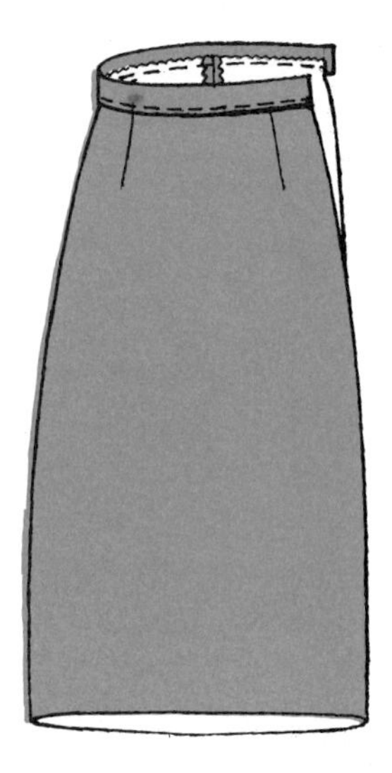

Check the same fitting points as on the basic pattern to be sure the skirt hangs as it should. If there are any minor adjustments to be made, such as making the waist or hip a little tighter, pin them in now. If a fold forms under the waistband, pin it for correcting later.

Slip the jacket on; fit the jacket over the skirt, and over a blouse or sweater, if you intend to wear one with the suit. You'll be surprised at how much ease a sweater can take up inside a jacket.

The center front of the jacket should be marked with basting thread so it can be lapped correctly for fitting. Pin it carefully down the

front. Check it at all points where you made adjustments on your basic muslin, and make sure the same adjustments have been correctly made in the suit. Remember, too, that the suit will have a lining, so the jacket should fit a little easy. (See lining information on page 57.) Mark the most becoming jacket length.

If any additional fitting is needed, again check the information already given on fitting. If the shoulders are too wide, for instance, pin a tuck from the shoulder down toward the bust, bringing the sleeve to the correct shoulder point. After you have finished fitting the suit jacket, rip out the sleeves and recut the shoulder width from the corrected jacket pattern.

Make additional adjustments the

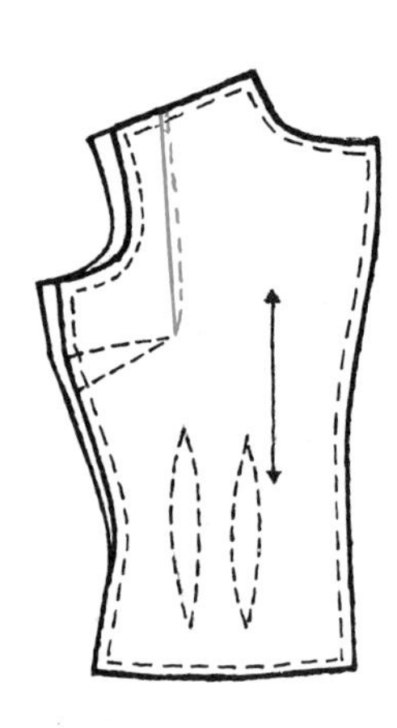

same way. Pin them in as you do on the basic pattern, and recut piece from the adjusted pattern.

Check the hang of the sleeve. It should hang so up-and-down grain and cross-grain are both straight. The slight crease you pressed in the sleeve will help in the fitting.

If any of the seams or darts need to be changed, you can rip and re-sew them without leaving a mark, since they have not been pressed.

Make all the corrections on the suit. Remove the basting from the seams, and your suit is ready for pressing. Leave the sleeves off until the jacket is finished; put the sleeves in as the last step.

Pressing

You'll need a tailor's ham to press your suit properly. (See instructions for making one on page 6.)

Use the wide part of the ham for shaping and molding both the hip and bustline. Always place the narrow end of the ham toward the waistline as you press a garment.

It's usually more convenient to press with the ham on a sleeve board, which makes it slightly higher. If you are short, this may not be a comfortable working position, and you will want to use the ham on the ironing board instead.

First, place the shoulder seam of the suit so it shapes along the edge of the wide end of the ham. Mold and press shoulder so that the back

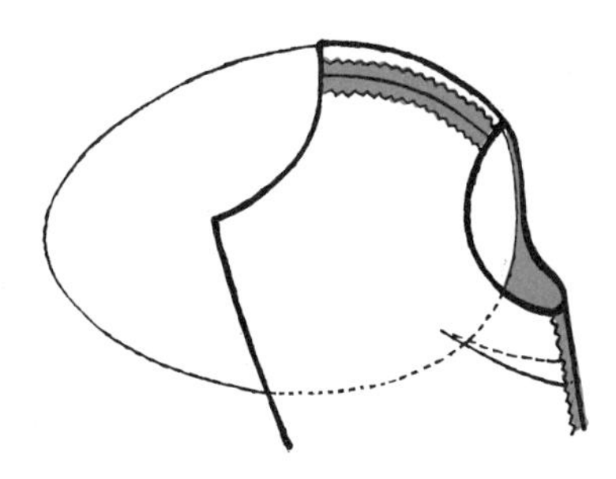

curves around the edge of the cushion as it will fit the curve of the back shoulder. This actually stretches back slightly along shoulder seam.

After you've pressed it, the front shoulder will be concave as you hold it over your hand. The back shoulder will follow the curve of the back of your hand, just as suit jacket will fit the back shoulder.

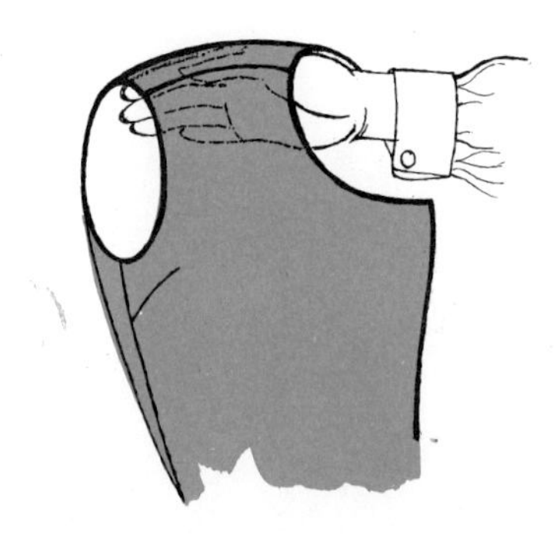

If the shoulder is sewed correctly, then molded as described, the suit back will never look too narrow. The sleeve will not pull toward the back, which too often happens on a homemade suit.

Next, press the underarm seam open, with the wide part of the ham toward the bustline. Press the darts on the ham, molding and shaping the roundness of the bustline. Press

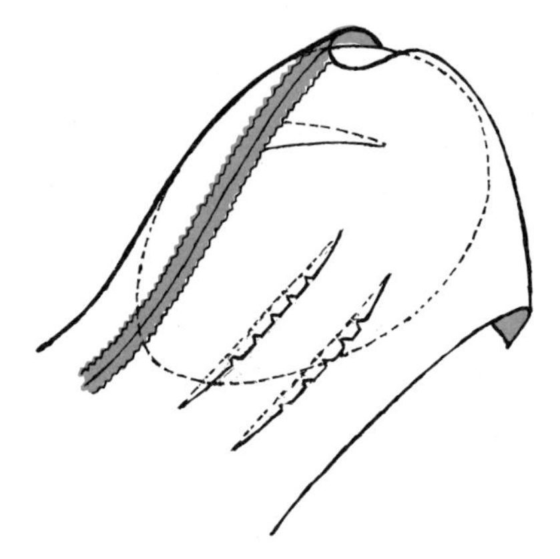

the hipline next, molding it over the wide part of the ham. The hip rounds out, following the shaping of the side seam and jacket darts.

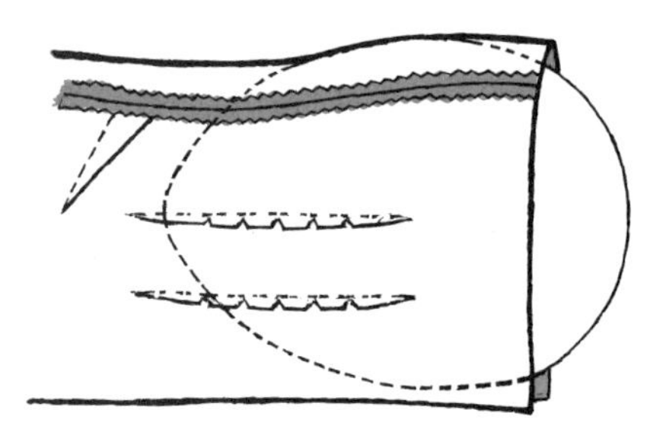

Press the same way on the back, first with the wide part of the ham toward the top to shape the upper back and shoulders, then toward the

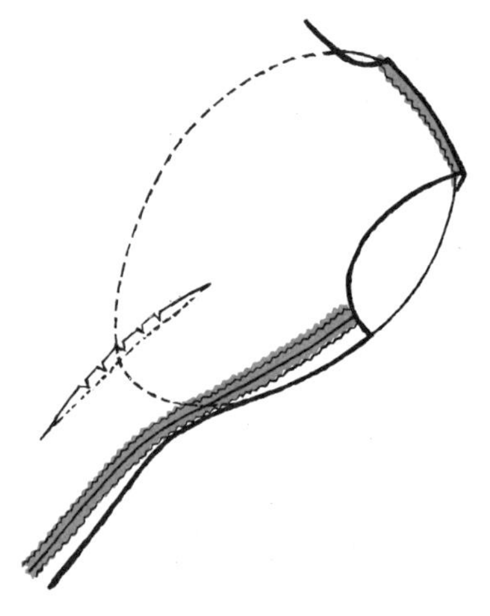

hip to round and mold the hipline.

When pressing your suit at the waistline, it is necessary to clip in on the waistline darts and seams, if the suit is a fitted style.

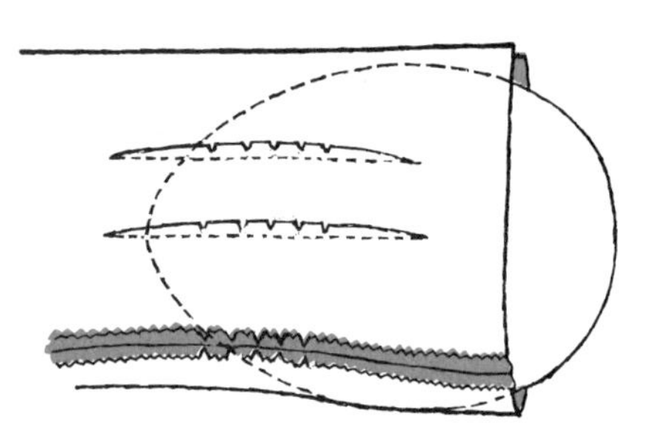

On the box-type jacket, you will only need to mold the shoulders, the bustline, and upper back of the suit jacket over the tailor's ham. The rest of the jacket can be pressed flat on a regular ironing board.

Interfacing

The front of the jacket is now ready to be interfaced.

For a suit with a *set-in sleeve,* cut the interfacing to extend out to the shoulder. Usually, the pattern includes a separate pattern piece for the interfacing. If the facing pattern piece is used, with extension added for cutting the interfacing, a slight change must be made. Cut the extension for the shoulder the same as the pattern, but add an extra inch on inside edge of the facing.

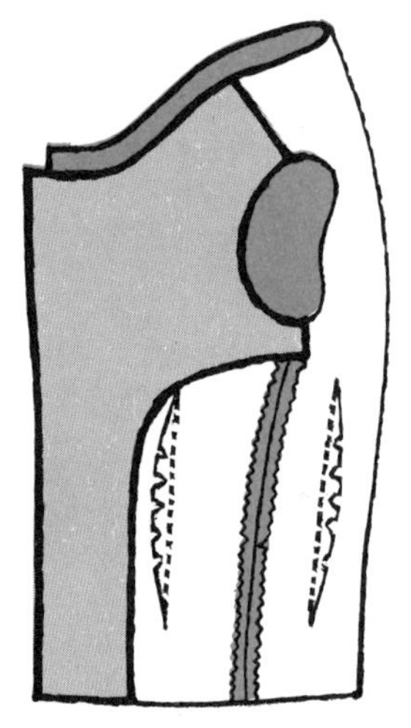

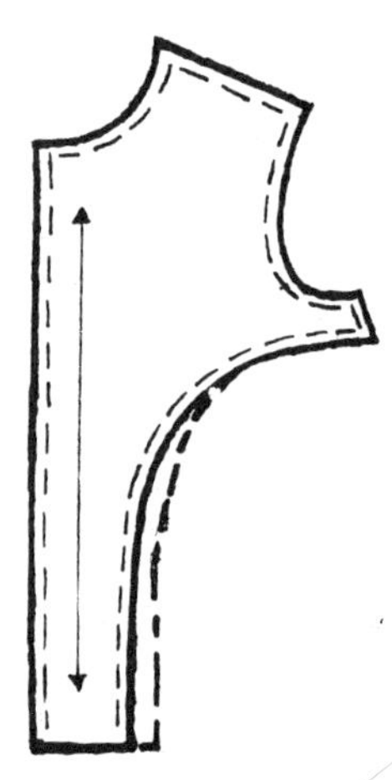

The interfacing should always be at least 1 inch wider than facing. If no interfacing pattern is included, use the jacket pattern front. Cut along front, shoulders, and armholes of jacket pattern.

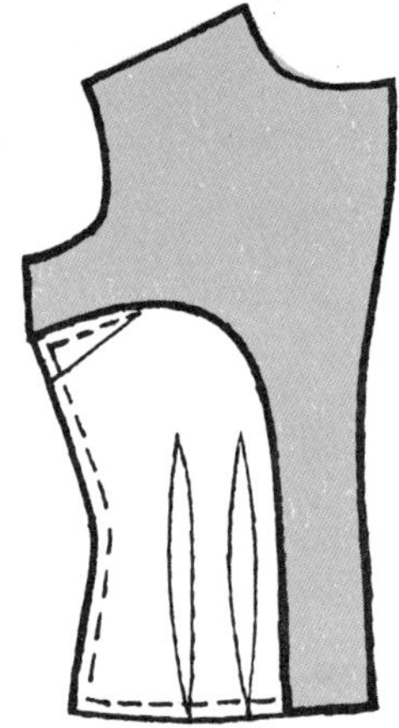

As you cut inside edge of interfacing, extend it 1 inch beyond where the facing would finish, and curve the interfacing just over the bust and to the side seams about 3 inches below the armhole.

On a suit with a *dolman sleeve,* cut the interfacing only 1 inch wider than the facing. The interfacing does not extend into the shoulder, since the shoulder is soft and it is molded to fit the figure.

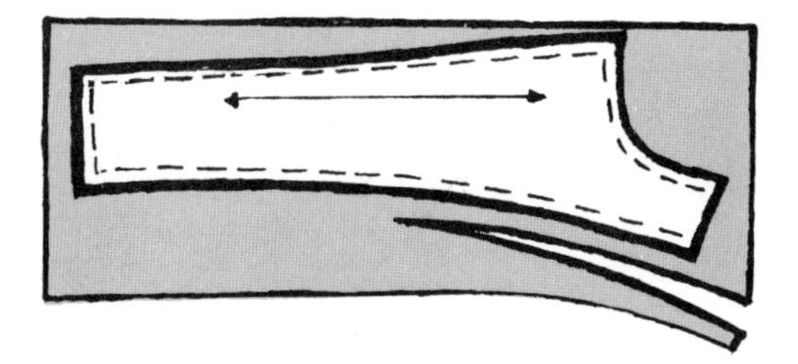

Cut the interfacing from hair canvas. Then fit it into the suit jacket around the armhole, the neck edge, and along the inside edge.

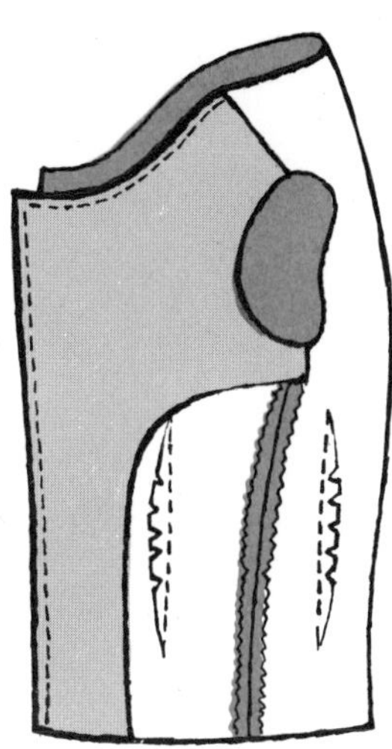

Place the suit over a tailor's ham, positioning it with the right side out. Mold and shape the suit over the ham to be sure that the interfacing fits smoothly to the inside. Then, from the right side, baste the interfacing into the suit along the shoulder seam, around the armhole seam, and down the inside edge of the suit jacket interfacing. Run another basting stitch from the center of the neckline straight down the front of the jacket to the suit jacket hem, catching interfacing.

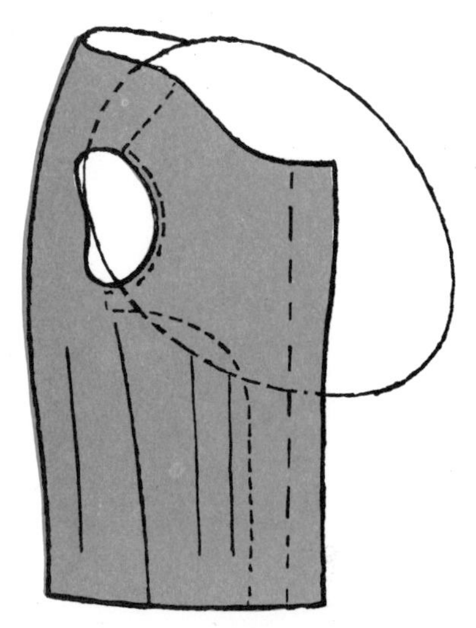

Take the front pattern piece and mark on right jacket front where the top buttonhole is to be placed.

Mark it exactly where the pattern indicates, because it will serve as a guide for the roll line. Mark it with a short basting thread. Mark the left side of the jacket in the same

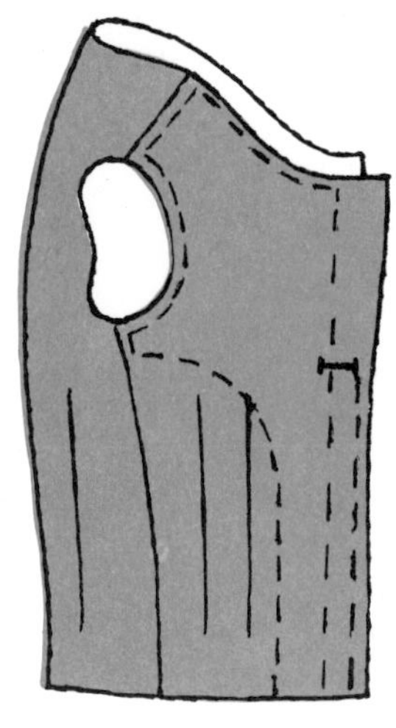

way. Baste the lower part of the interfacing to the jacket along front edge to the buttonhole mark.

Now you are ready for a crucial point in making any suit—the rolling of the lapel. The roll line runs from the outside edge of the buttonhole mark toward neckline between the shoulder and the center front.

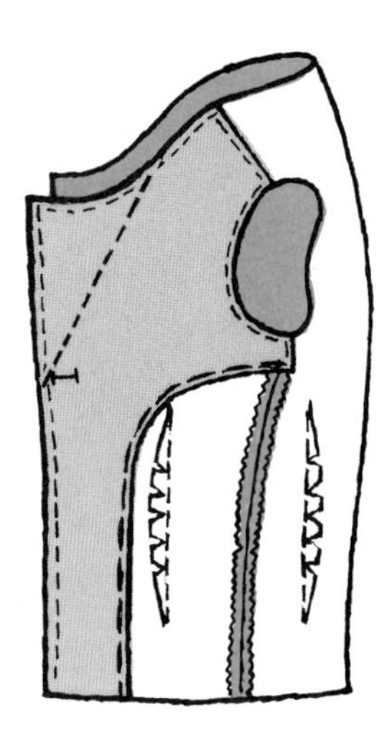

Rolling the lapel

Roll the lapel over your hand with the interfacing on top. Start a padding-stitch about 1 inch inside the roll line. Work the padding-stitch up and down lapel, inside the seam allowance line of the front edge and the neck edge. The stitches can be as fine and close together as you like. Suit lapel rolls over your hand as you work, so that roll will be sewed in permanently. Finish rolling the lapel on jacket fronts.

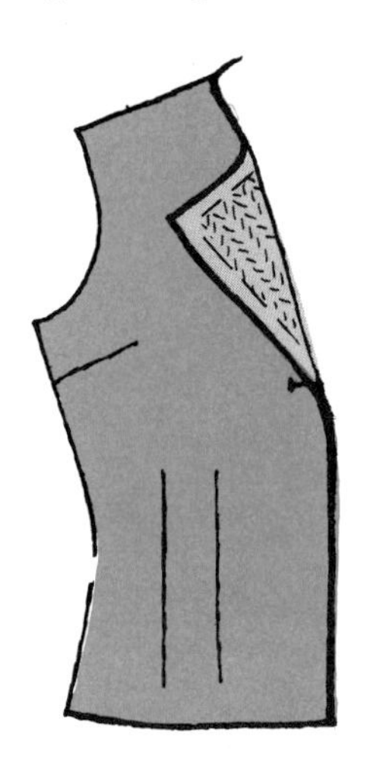

Trim away the seam allowance on the interfacing around front edge of the jacket and of the neck. The amount of seam allowance will vary, depending on how much was taken up in the rolling of the lapel. Be sure to leave slightly more than 5/8 inch seam allowance at the jacket edge.

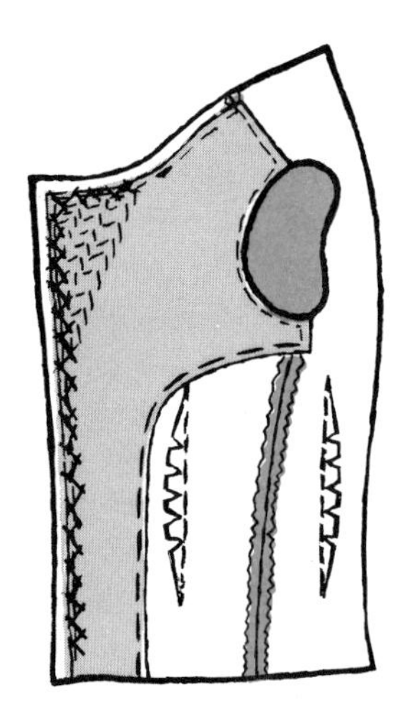

Now you are ready to sew the interfacing to the inside of the suit. Sew it by hand, using a catch-stitch around the front edge of the jacket and neck edge. Sew it to the shoulders and around the armhole with a running-stitch. On inside edge of interfacing, use a long catch-stitch, picking up only a few of the threads of the surface, so the stitching won't show on the right side. Make this stitch rather loose. If the suit jack-

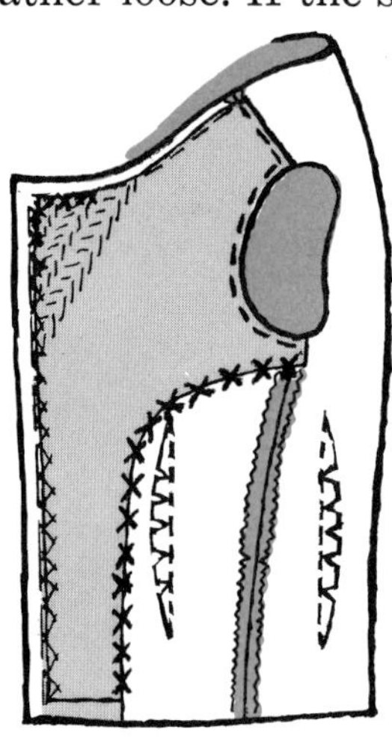

et is mounted, sew the interfacings only to the underlinings.

To interface the back of the suit, cut the interfacing on the bias from the back jacket pattern. The interfacing can be lightweight muslin or a commercial interfacing in a crisper finish. When cutting, follow the pattern at the neck edge, armhole, and to about 3 inches below the armhole at the side seam. Then curve across the back to about 5 inches below the neck. Sew the back interfacing by hand around the outside jacket edges. Interfacing is not tacked to body of suit, and the inside edge of interfacing hangs free.

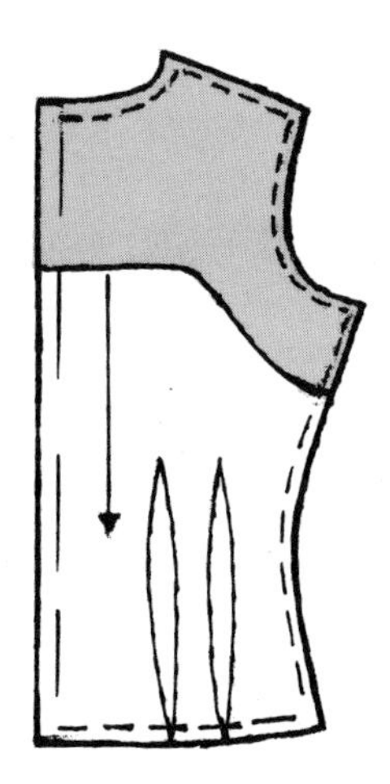

Taping

Always tape the front edge of the suit to keep it firm and to prevent stretching. A 1/4-inch linen tape is best. You can also use a 1/4-inch twill tape, but be sure it is preshrunk.

Baste the tape to the front edge of the suit along the seam allowance line and across the neck edge to the center front line. Also tape the width of the facing across the lower front edge on the hemline.

Baste the edges of the tape with a zigzag stitch. Keep it smooth and even along seam edge. Ease it in if it has to be shaped to any curve. Sew the tape permanently with a fine hemming-stitch along the seam edges. On the outside edge, pick up a few threads of fabric. Sew the inside edge to the interfacing only. Tape will extend slightly beyond front edge of the interfacing, since the seam allowance was cut to a little more than 5/8 inch.

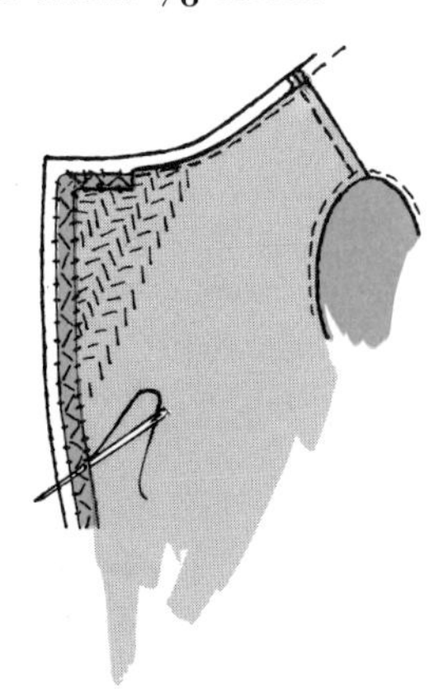

Buttonholes

Slip the suit jacket on and pin it together down the front. The top buttonhole has already been marked. Carefully indicate the front waistline. Put a pin 1/2 inch below it for placement of waistline buttonhole.

Remove jacket. Check the front jacket with the pattern piece to see whether placement of the waistline buttonhole is the same as the one marked on the actual pattern. If it is not, re-mark the waistline buttonhole on the pattern.

Measure and re-mark all buttonholes on jacket pattern front so they are evenly spaced between the top and waistline buttonholes. From this corrected pattern, make tracing from which you'll make all buttonholes. (See instructions for making cord-bound buttonhole in Creative Sewing Book on *Professional Sewing Tips.*)

Interfacing hipline and hem

The hemline of a jacket is generally interfaced to give a firm and smooth edge. You must consider the style of the suit in deciding how deep the interfacing should be. Sometimes the hipline of a suit is arched to give a rounded look at the hip. This must be interfaced to hold the shape—one of the nonwoven interfacings would be best. Cut the interfacing from the back and front suit pattern, following the lower edge of the jacket and cutting a little above the waistline mark shown on pattern.

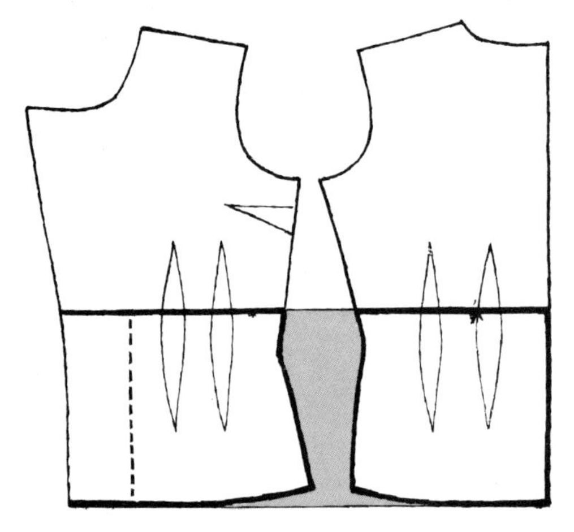

Sew up the side seams, press them open, then stitch about ¼ inch on either side of the seamline.

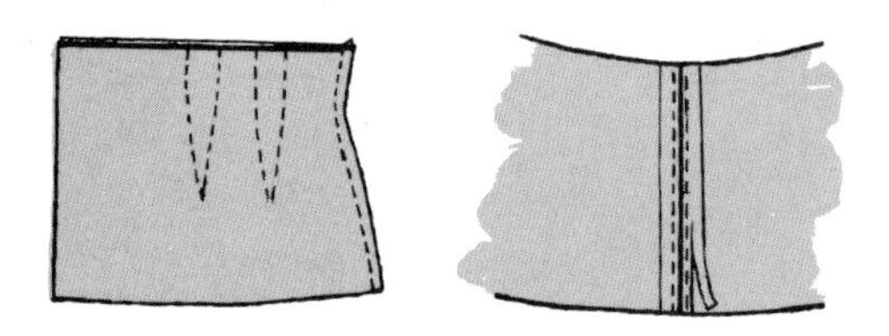

Cut out the center of the darts. Lap the edges together, put a strip of interfacing underneath. Stitch on each side of the cut edges to shape.

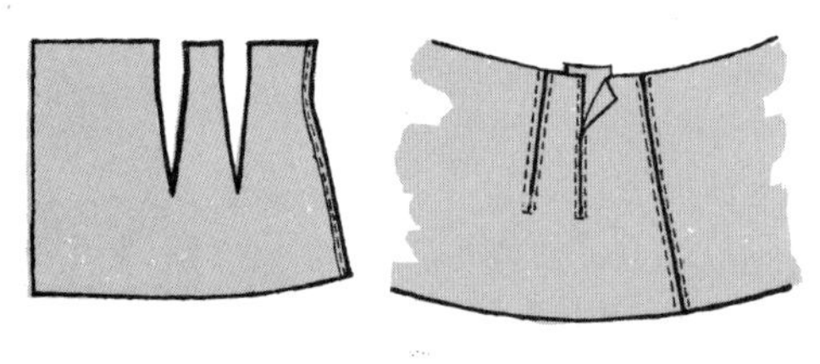

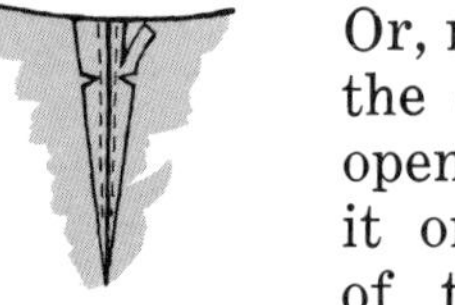

Or, mark and sew the dart, slash it open, and stitch it on either side of the seamline. This keeps the interfacing flat and smooth under the suit fabric, but gives the correct arch to the hip.

Press back the hem of the jacket.

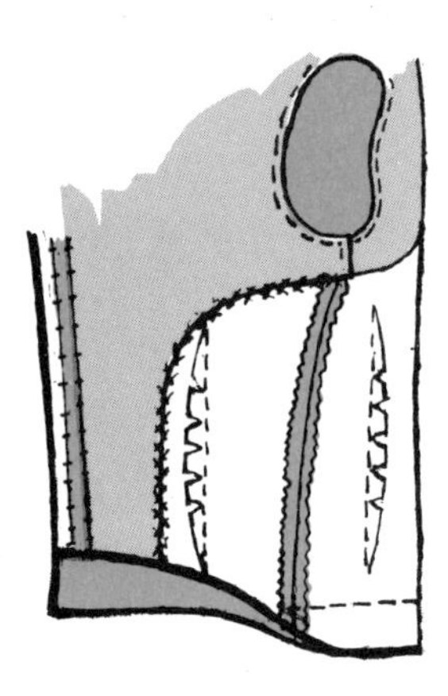

At lower edge, cut away the interfacing the width of the hem and fit it to the inside of jacket on the fold line of the hem. Pin the interfacing along back and front darts and the side seams. Cut off front of the hip interfacing so it just laps over the front interfacing.

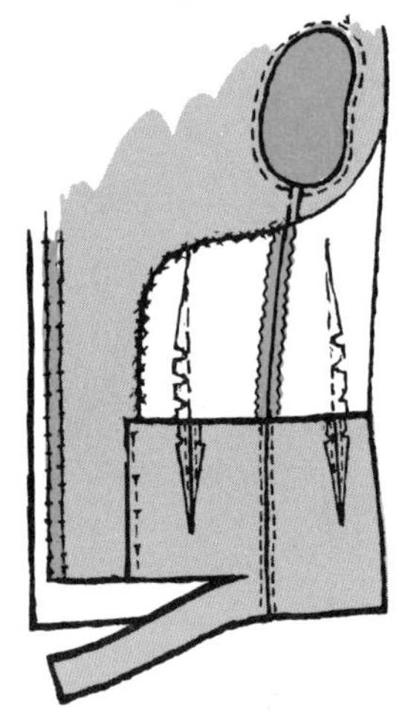

Catch-stitch the interfacing along the hem crease and at the top edge. On the seams and darts, do a running-stitch through the interfacing to the matching dart or seam. Be sure none of the tacking shows on the right side. If the entire hipline does not need interfacing, you need to do only the hem.

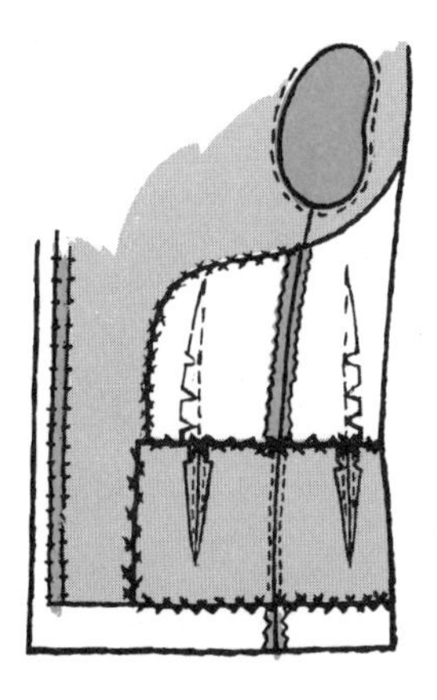

Cut the interfacing of hair canvas or of nonwoven interfacing. The hair canvas interfacing is cut on the bias, 1 inch wider than the depth of the hem. The nonwoven interfacing is cut 1 inch wider than the hem, and it is cut to the shape of the edge of the suit jacket. Both the hair canvas and nonwoven interfacings are sewed in the same way.

Pin the lower edge of the interfacing just inside the crease for the hem. Don't stretch the lower edge of the suit. Catch-stitch both edges of the interfacing to the suit. Be sure no stitching shows on the right

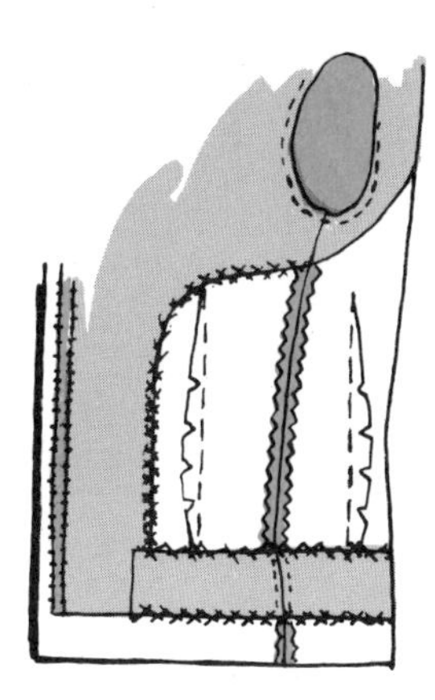

side of the jacket when you finish.

When the jacket has been mounted on an underlining, baste the underlining to jacket on the hemline before pressing back hem. Leave basting in until suit is completed.

Collars

Notched collar

This collar has a notch where it joins the neck seam. The under collar is always cut in two pieces on the bias and with a center seam, so it will roll softly and uniformly, and be easier to mold under upper collar.

Cut the interfacing on the bias from the canvas, using the same pattern as for the under collar.

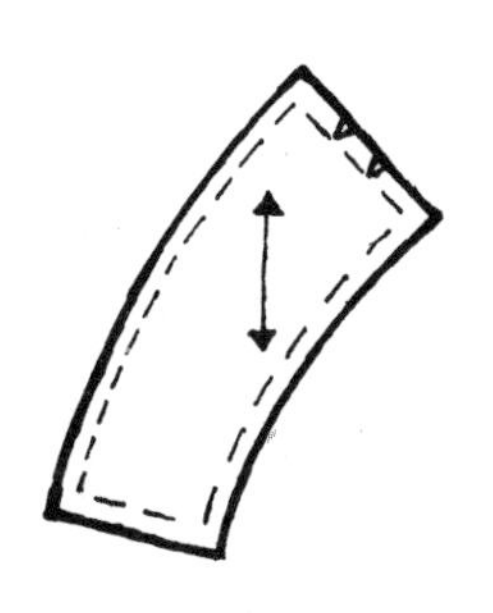

Sew up the center seam of the under collar and press the seam open.

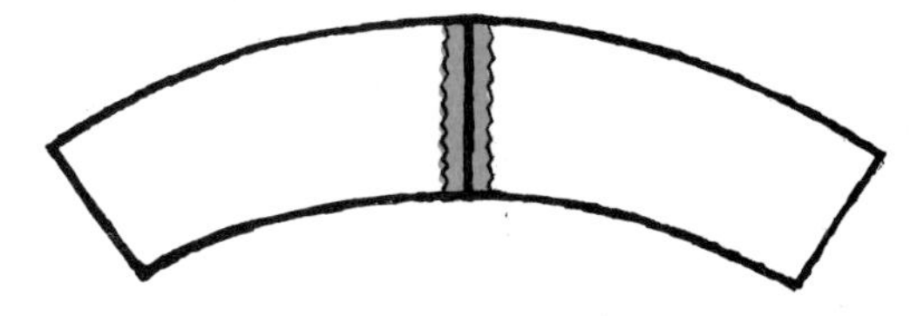

On the interfacing, press open the seam, and then stitch on either side of it to hold seam allowances flat. Cut off seams close to the stitching.

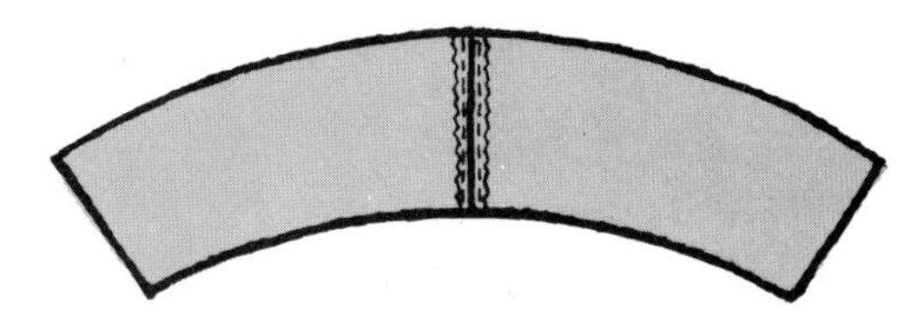

Place the interfacing against the inside of the under collar and pin to hold the center seams together.

This collar must have roll line

sewed in. Do this by hand, using thread the color of the suit.

Start at the neck seam allowance line, ½ inch to the side of the center seam. Use the same padding-stitch that you used for the lapel. Roll the collar over your index finger and start the padding-stitch, forming a small-size circle in the center of the notched collar.

As you do the padding, ease the interfacing in slightly, while rolling the collar over your finger. Work from one side of the collar to the other, making an ever-widening circle. Do the padding-stitch only to the seam allowance line all around.

Finish the center of the collar. Then continue the padding-stitch on either side of the collar, from the outside edge to the neck edge, until you've completely padded the collar.

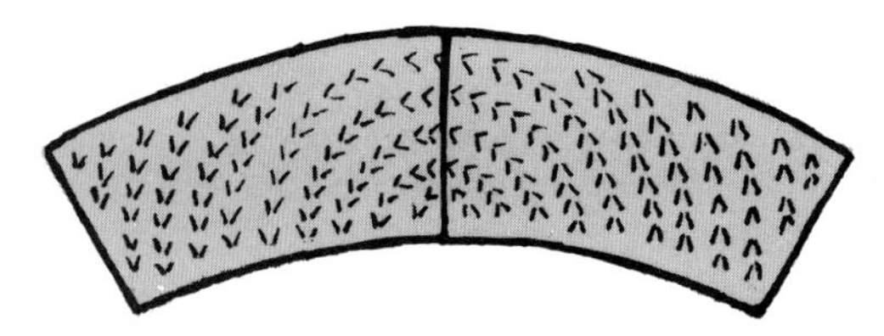

If the interfacing has been eased in enough, you may find that there is very little seam allowance left on the interfacing. In any case, trim

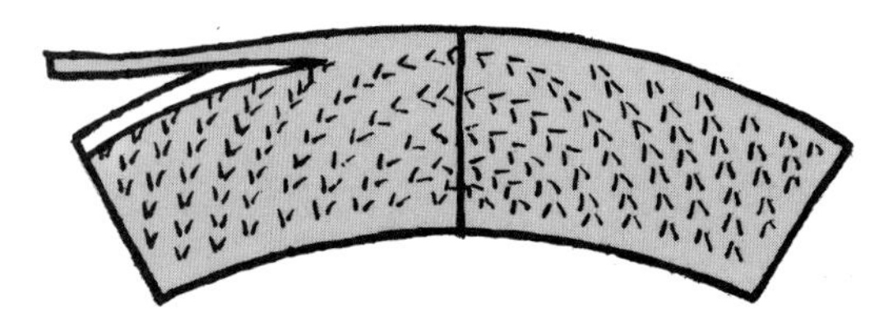

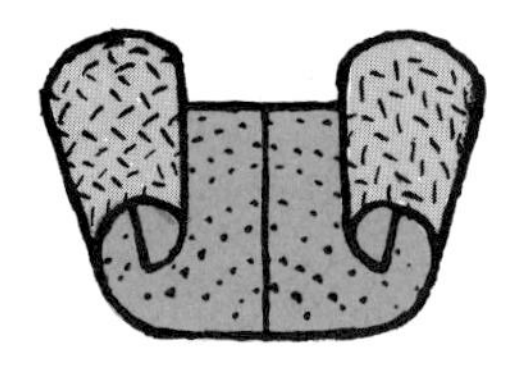

away the interfacing to the seam allowance line all around the collar. When rolled correctly, ends will curl toward the under collar.

The collar is now ready to be applied to the suit. First, put a stay-stitch in the neckline to keep it from stretching and to permanently hold neck size. Tape is never used as a stay in necklines and armholes of fine custom suits. Always stay-stitch necklines and armholes by hand.

Stay-stitching the neck

Use a single strand of silk buttonhole twist for this stitching. Start at the center front of the neck, or where the collar will be sewed.

Bring the needle through from the inside of the neck, just outside the seam allowance line. Then take a back-stitch ½ inch long, and bring the needle forward ¼ inch, next to original stitch. The needle should always come out at the top of the stitching line. Draw in on the thread slightly before you take the next ½ inch back-stitch. Do this

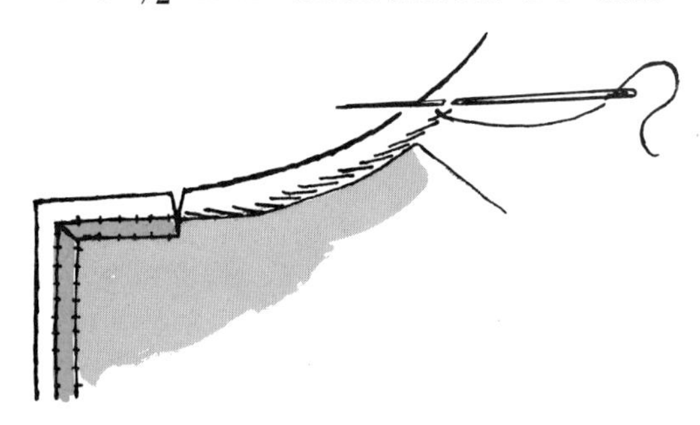

stitch all around the neckline. Measure carefully to be sure the neck is same size as your pattern piece.

This stitching can be done in the same color thread as the suit, or in a contrasting color. You may find the contrasting thread color is easier to see when sewing the collar.

Now you will see how important it is to notch the front of the neck where the collar joins the jacket.

Pin the front of the collar to the jacket so the seam allowance line is at this notch at both sides of the neckline. Match the center back of the under collar to the center back of the neck. Pin the rest of the collar to the neckline all around on the seam allowance line, matching neckline notches. The stay-stitching at the neck can serve as a guide on the jacket; trimmed-off interfacing indicates seamline on collar.

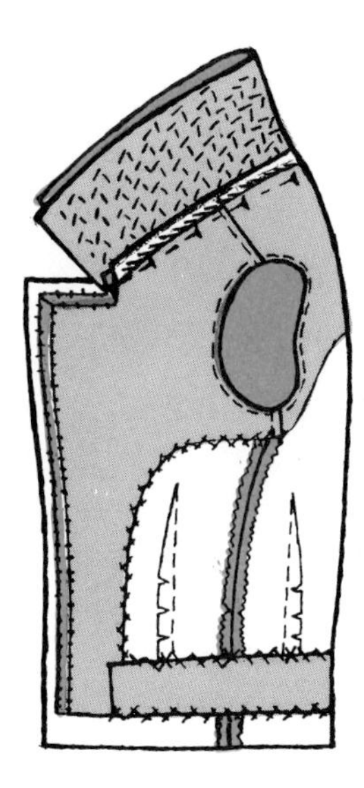

Stitch the collar to the neck. Remember to sew back a few stitches to securely lock the stitching where

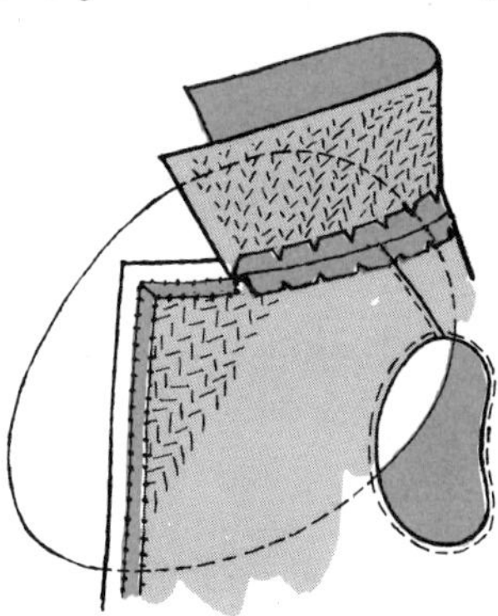

the suit collar finishes to either end.

Clip in to the neckline stitching at this point. Clip in on the neck seam and press it open all around. Press the neckline over a tailor's ham so the neckline will not be stretched during the pressing.

Facing and upper collar

Join the upper collar to the facing. Collar and facings can be sewed to the suit in one stitching.

Mark the notches carefully on both pieces before removing the pattern. Also mark by clipping where the collar joins facing to form the notch. If collar has a mark indicating where it matches shoulder seam, also clip it at this mark.

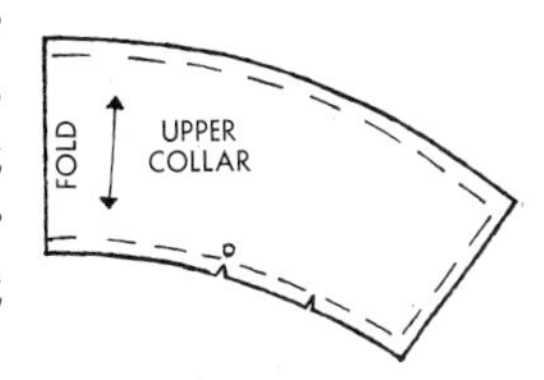

Pin the collar to the facing, matching the seam allowance line of the collar to the clip mark on facing.

If the collar is marked for the shoulder seam, pin at the seam allowance line at the top of the facing. Be sure to match the neckline notches of facing and collar. Sew the two pieces together along seamline.

Ease the collar in a little around the curve of the front neck. Sew back a few stitches at the front edge of the collar to lock it. Clip in to the stitching line at this point. Clip in to the curve seam of the neck and carefully press the seam open.

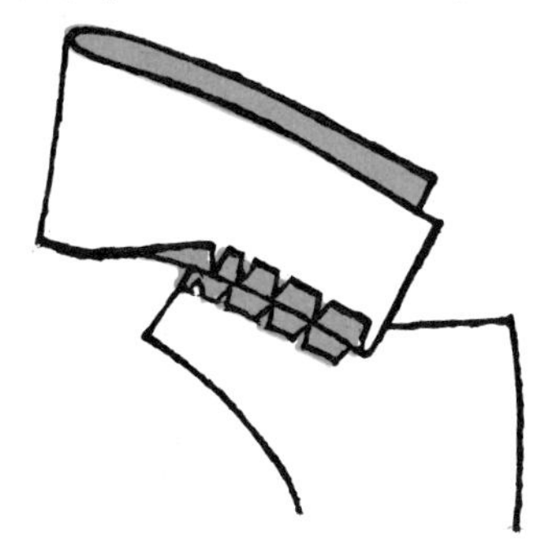

Bring the right side of the collar and the facing to the right side of the suit, with edges of the collars and facing together, and the neckline seams directly over each other. Baste neckline seams together, easing in the facing side slightly.

Pin the facing and collar to the suit and under collar along the interfacing. Or, you can pin at the seam allowance line.

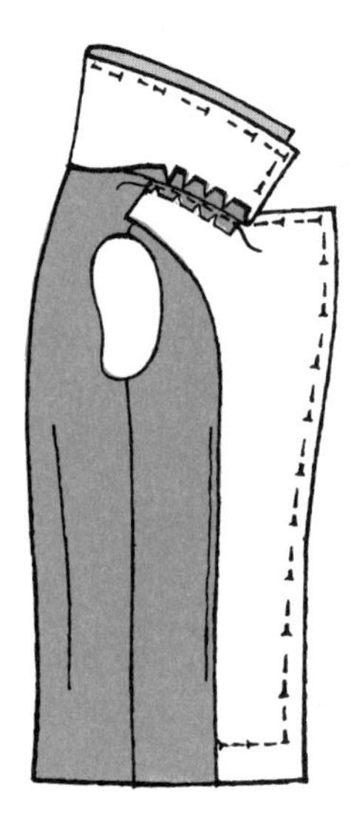

Ease the facing in slightly along the top of the lapel. As you pin the front edges of the suit together, ease the facing slightly along the lapel line. Also you should ease the upper collar at the front edges and for the entire length.

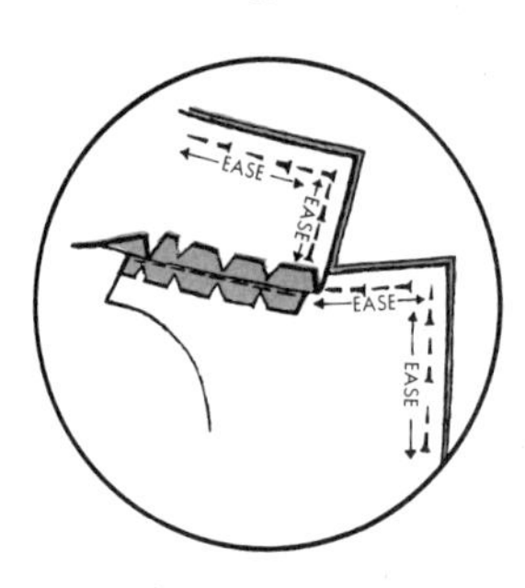

Start to sew from the right-hand side of the suit on the inside, and from the bottom of the jacket to the back of collar. Do the same thing from the left-hand side of jacket.

This keeps the ease from shifting as it might if you sewed all around the jacket. It also assures that the lapels will roll the same way.

When you sew into the notch, be sure to sew just to the base of the clip mark, and then up the side of the collar on seam allowance line.

This part of the notch can often be spread open, so the collar and the top lapel seam are in a straight line. Stitching it in this way sometimes helps to insure that the collar notch is sewed correctly.

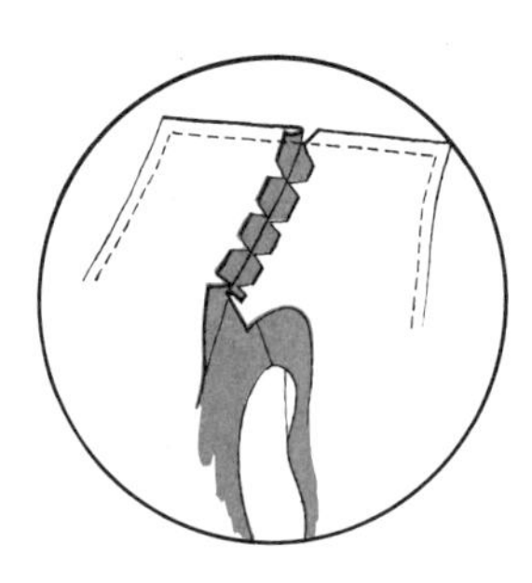

When the facings are turned to the inside, the top edge of the lapel should look as if it is a continuous part of the neck seam. Your suit collar should be at a direct angle to this neck seam. Turn the facing, and check at this point to be sure that it has been sewed correctly.

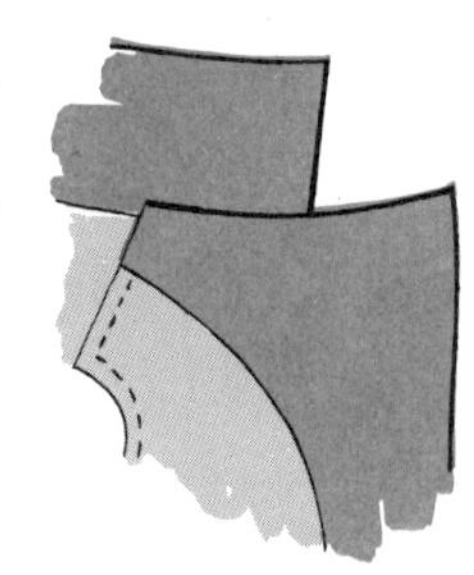

If the notch is correct, trim the seam to graduated widths. Make the suit seam quite narrow, the facing slightly wider. Trimming the seams this way makes the front edge of the

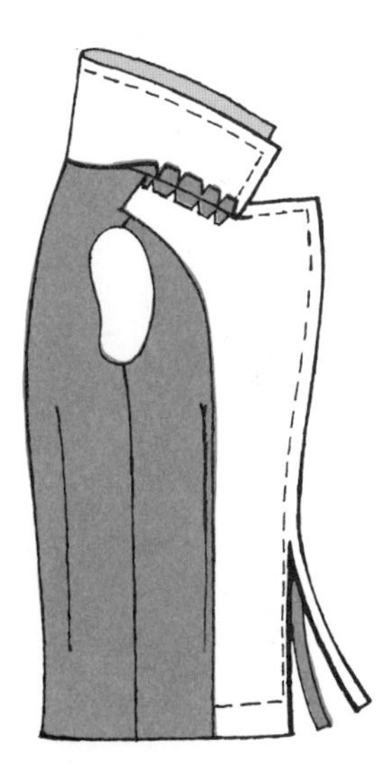

jacket flat and smooth. Turn the facing to the inside, and baste around the edge of the suit. At the lower front edge of the suit jacket, you should bring the facing in just slightly from the seamline edge.

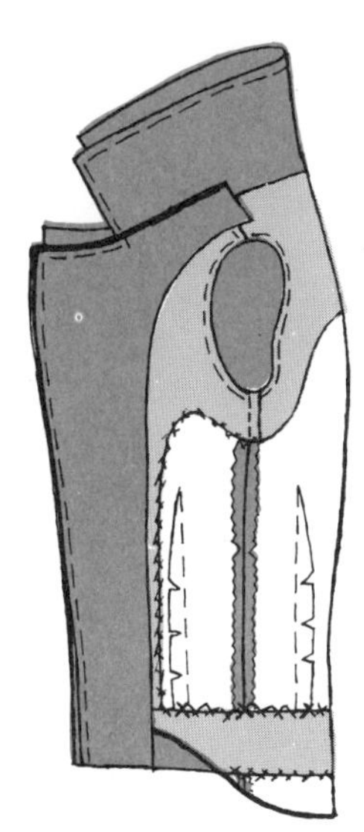

As you baste around the lapel, bring the suit back a little from the seam edge. Baste the under collar so its edge is also in just slightly from seamline. This is done so you are not pressing collar on seamline, but on a fold of fabric along the front edge of the suit. This gives a sharper line, an invisible seam.

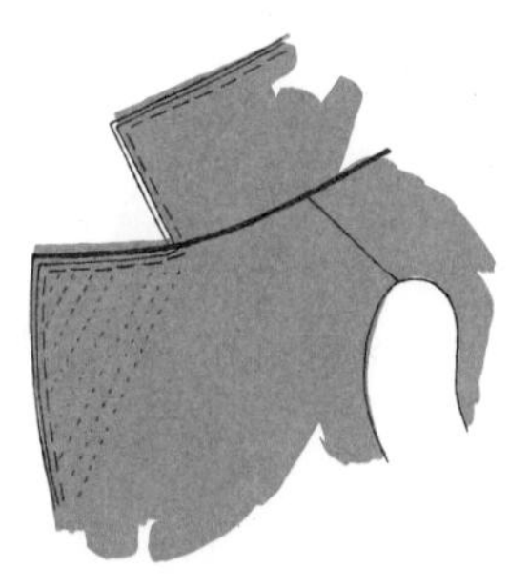

On lightweight fabrics, as the facing is sewed around the collar and lapel, it can also be sewed across the hemline. Then when it is turned, the lower edge of the suit jacket is finished at the same time. With a

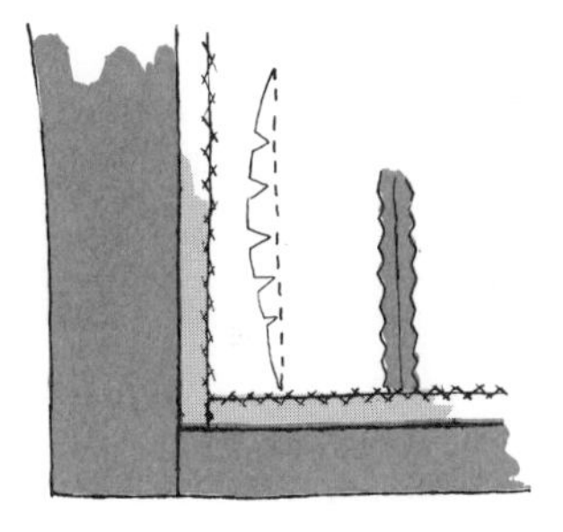

heavier fabric, turn up the hem and turn under the facing. Finish by hand; as the facing is tacked to jacket, under hem can be cut away.

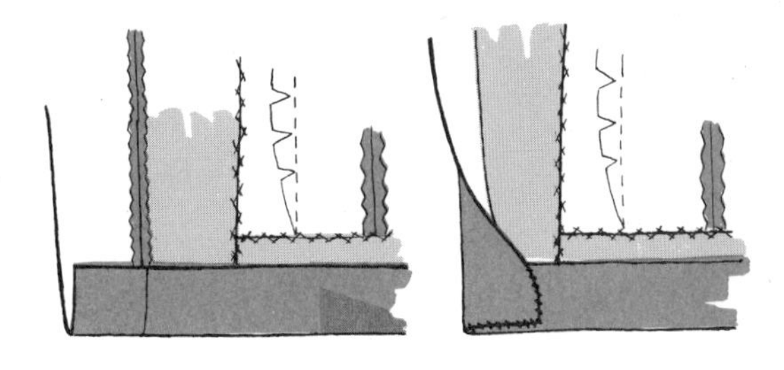

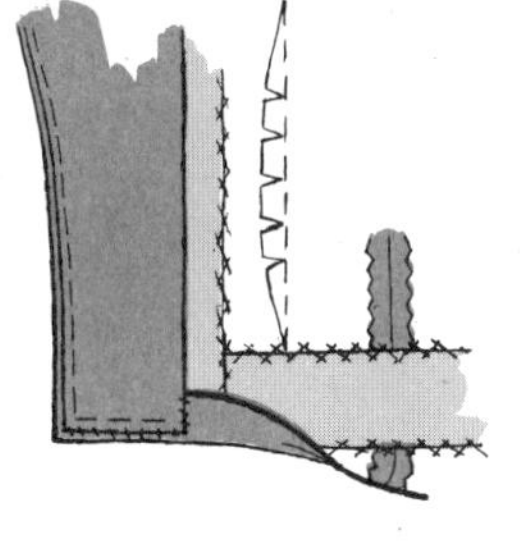

Press the facings back on the inside at the lower part of the suit jacket, as it was basted. Then press the lapel on the suit side. Press the collar on the under collar side. Do all pressing over a tailor's ham.

Roll collar and lapel over your hand. Then do a diagonal basting all along the roll line, as you hold two thicknesses in place as they will roll. Put the right side of jacket down on ham, smooth back lower facings and pin into place. Now roll

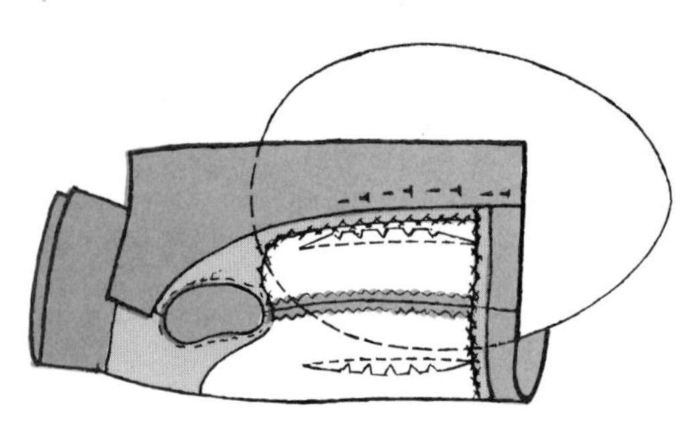

back the lapel and place it face down on the ham. Then smooth back the upper part of the facing and pin to the inside of the suit. The lapel is rolled under first, so the ease in the collar and facings will not be pulled to the inside of the suit when the collar and facings are finished.

If smoothed back too much, the ease would be eliminated, spoiling the roll of the collar and the lapel.

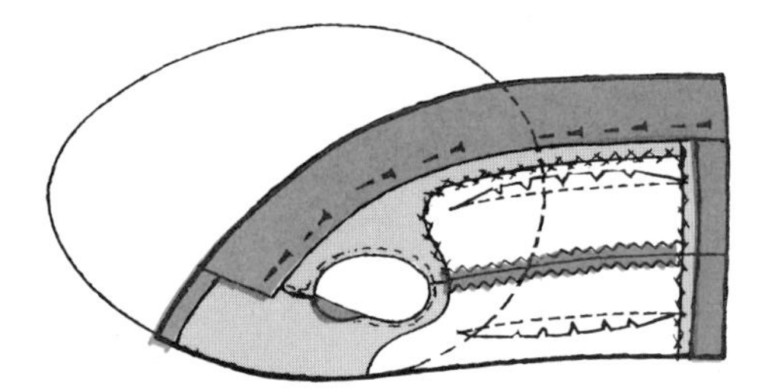

Roll upper collar back and pin loose edge to the back neckline.

Be sure the upper collar has sufficient ease so that it will roll over the under collar and set correctly.

Do a running-stitch around the collar and shoulder to hold in place. On the facings and hem, catch-stitch the edges to the interfacing.

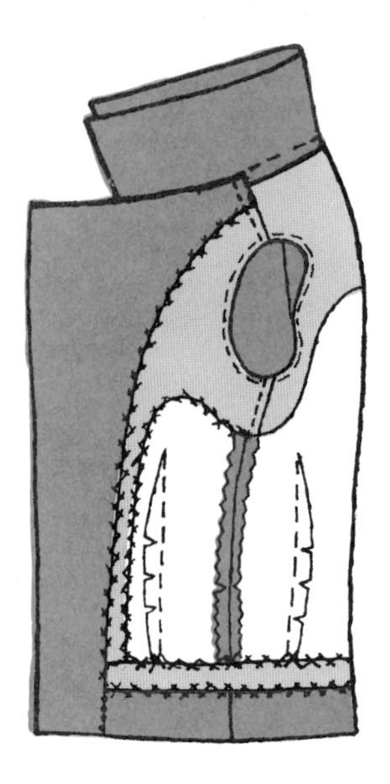

Reasons that a collar "dog-ears" are (1) because not enough easing was done when upper collar, facings were sewed to suit, (2) facings and collar were finished to inside without allowing ease where collar, lapel roll over under collar and lapel.

Shawl collar

There are two ways the shawl collar can be constructed. It's a good idea to know how to make both, since different patterns show both ways.

The first method is to cut the under collar in one piece with the front of the suit jacket, cutting the upper collar in one piece with the facing.

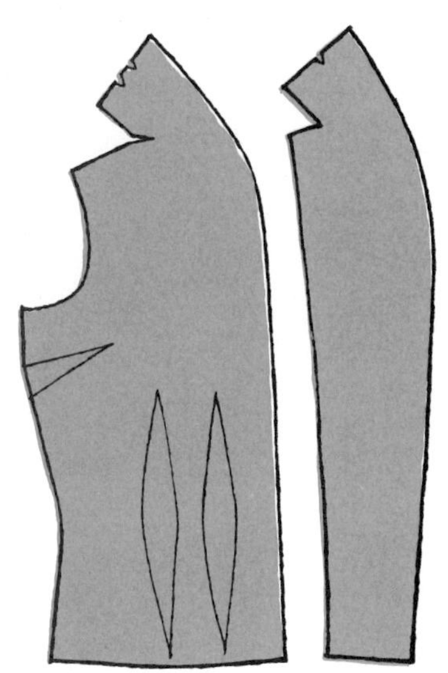

The interfacing will also be cut with collar and facing in a single piece. Cut interfacing from hair canvas, one inch wider than facing. Sew up back neck seam. Trim away seam allowance at the back of the neck and at the top shoulder of the interfacing.

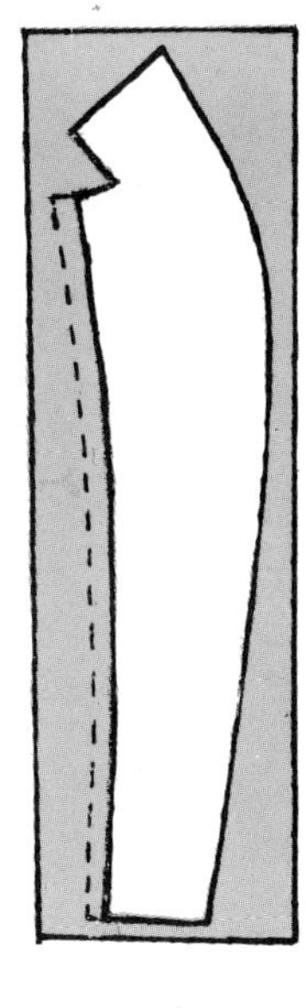

Then carefully pin this edge to the seamline of neck and shoulder of the suit. Smooth the interfacing into the inside of the suit and pin edges to

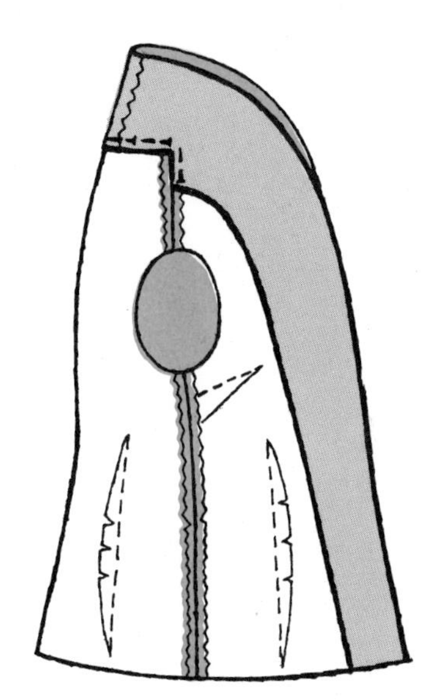

jacket. Roll the collar back from the mark of the first buttonhole to the back of the neck, as you do when making a notched collar. Put pins along the roll line to hold it. Smooth the interfacing into the inside of the suit and pin inside edges to jacket.

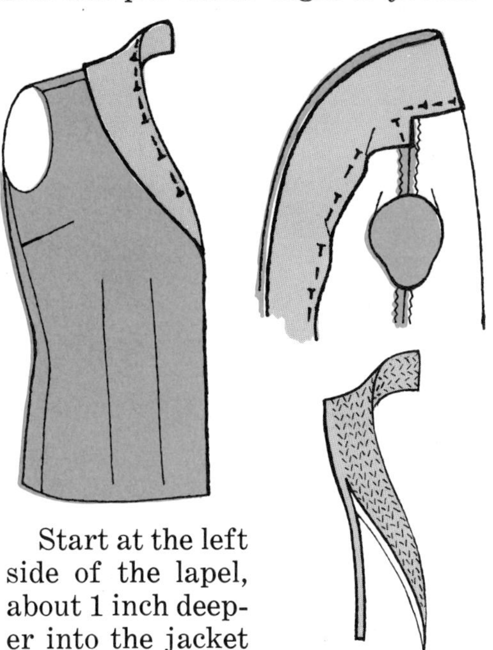

Start at the left side of the lapel, about 1 inch deeper into the jacket than the roll line, and begin to make a padding-stitch.

Work back and forth around the collar and lapel until the entire collar is padded to the seam allowance line at the collar edge.

Trim the interfacing at the seam allowance line. Catch interfacing to the neck with a running-stitch across the back neck and shoulder seam. Then, catch-stitch rest of interfacing to the inside of jacket, as for a notched collar style suit. Use tape as for a notched collar on front suit edge to top buttonhole mark. Never tape around collar.

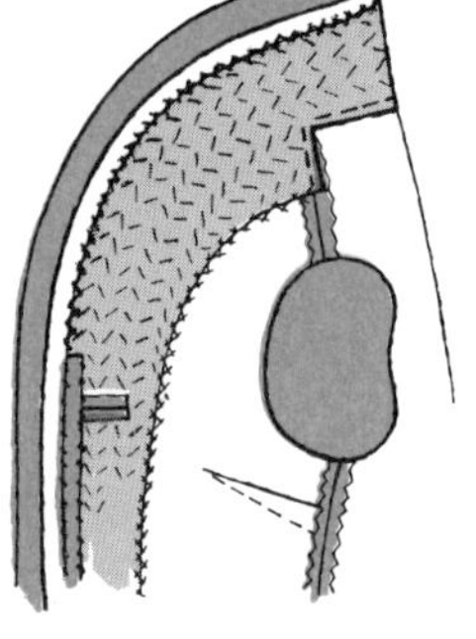

Facings

Join the back collar seam of the facings and press. Next, pin the right side of the facing to the right side of your suit jacket.

Ease the facing around the collar and lapel. Pin on the suit side along the edge of the interfacing.

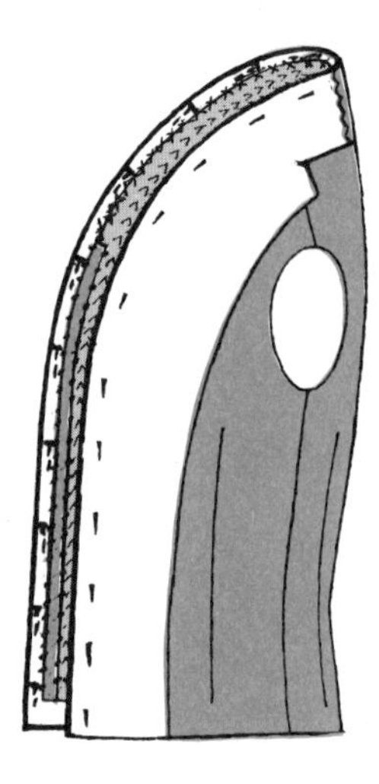

Stitch the facing to one side of the suit from the hem to the back neck. Then stitch the other side of the suit from the hem to back neck. This keeps the facing ease from shifting, as it is stitched. The roll of the collar will be same on both sides. Trim the front seam allowances to graduated widths. Turn the facing to the inside. Baste the edge of the collar and facings for pressing. On the lower front of the jacket, bring the facing in slightly from the seam

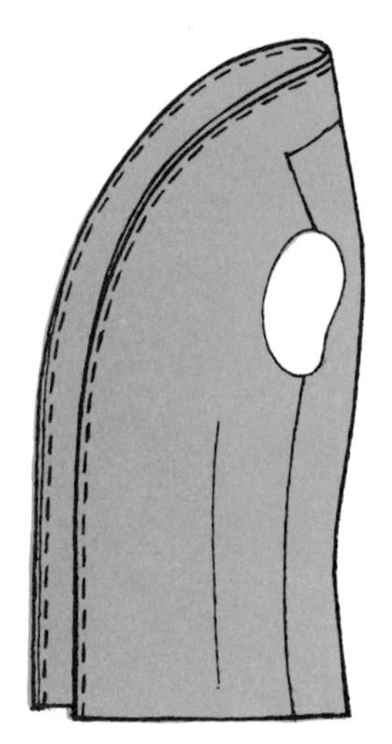

edge and baste. Press the front edge carefully. Press the lower edge of the jacket on the facing side. Now press around the collar on the suit side. Before you tack facing to inside of the jacket, roll the collar over your hand and do a diagonal basting stitch all around collar to hold it at the roll line. At the lower front of the jacket, smooth the facing to the inside and pin the edges to the jacket. Roll the collar and lapel back, then smooth the facing to the inside. When the collars are rolled back before the facings are

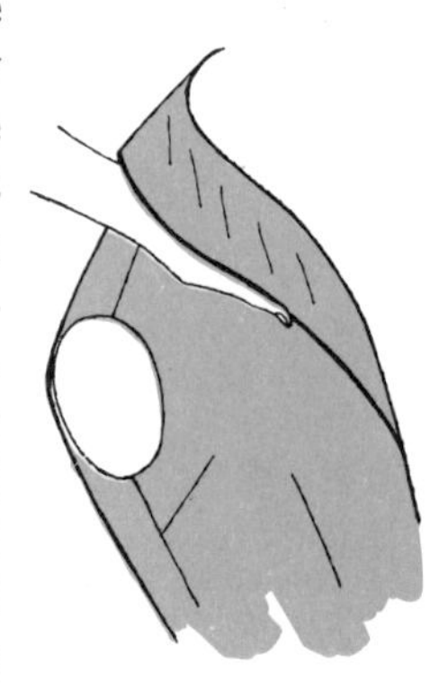

tacked, the roll line won't be spoiled. Catch-stitch the facings to the inside as you do on a notched collar.

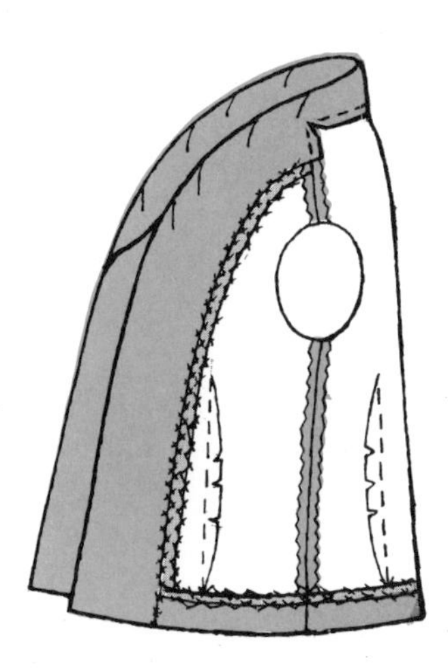

The second method for making the shawl collar is to make the under collar as a separate piece and sew it to the jacket, forming the shape of the shawl collar. The facing and

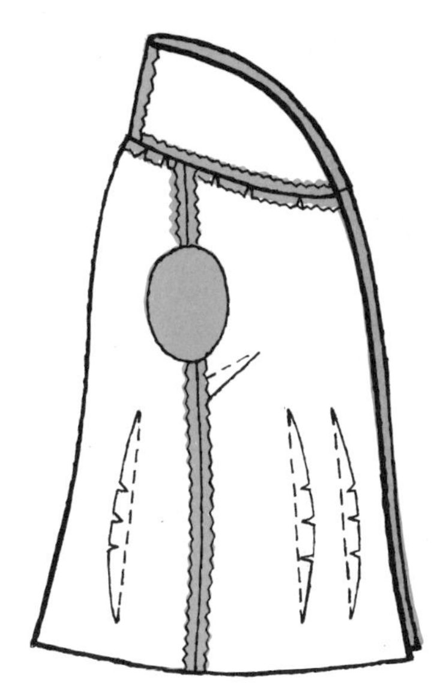

upper collar are cut in one piece as in the other construction. On this second style, interface the collar and suit front separately, as you do on a notched-collar suit. After the collar is sewed to the suit, apply the facing as for a regular shawl collar.

Shawl collar with a notch

This collar can be constructed like either of the shawl collars just described. Along the lapel on the pattern, you will find a notch marked to simulate a regular notched collar, or to provide a trim.

Mark the exact placement of the notches on both lapels of the suit. You can do this with a basting-stitch. Follow the same procedure in making either of the shawl collars. Only difference is you must cut away interfacing around notch mark.

When the edge of the suit is taped, be sure to run the tape around the edges of this notch, so notch will remain firm. Miter the tape at the points, but at inside corner, fold it to the reverse side, thus forming a perfect corner. Sew the tape to the

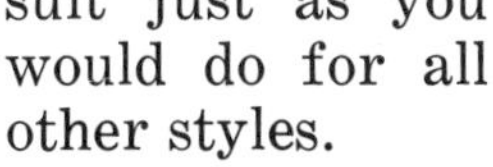

suit just as you would do for all other styles.

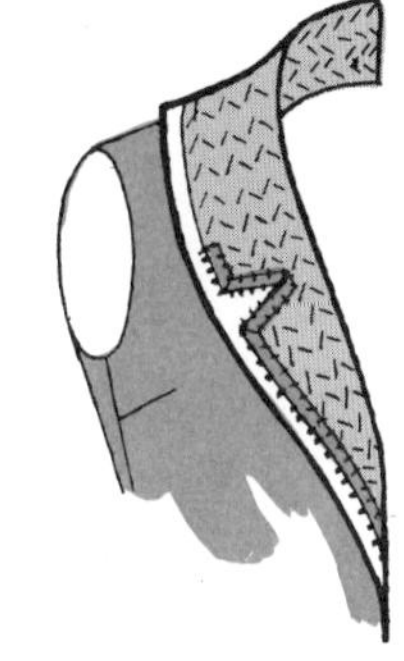

Cardigan-type jacket

This jacket is easy to make, since

it has no collar to be applied and rolled. After the suit is assembled and fitted, cut interfacings of hair canvas or nonwoven interfacing. The interfacing extends into shoulder, as in suit with set-in sleeve.

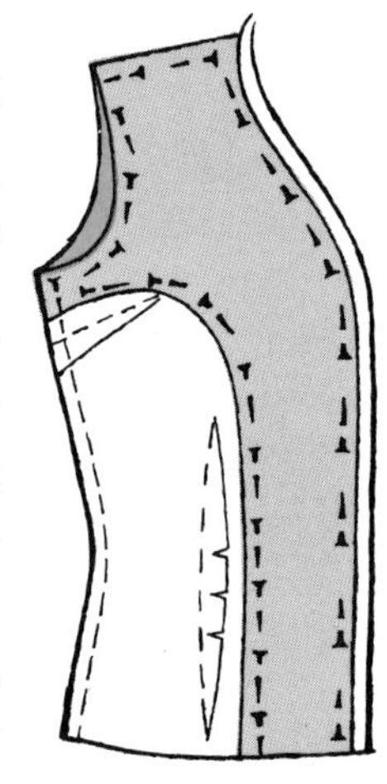

Cut off seam allowance at front edge and neck of the cardigan. Fit it to the inside of the suit jacket, with the edge of the interfacing at the seam allowance line of the front edge of your suit.

Now pin around the edges and into suit jacket.

To interface the back neck, cut the interfacing piece one inch wider than the back facing piece. Cut off the seam allowance at the neck. Fit the interfacing into the back of the jacket. Lap the interfacing at the shoulder line. Then, catch-stitch the edges of the interfacings to the jacket. Now add interfacing at the jacket hem, as shown on page 19. Pin facing to the suit. Then sew

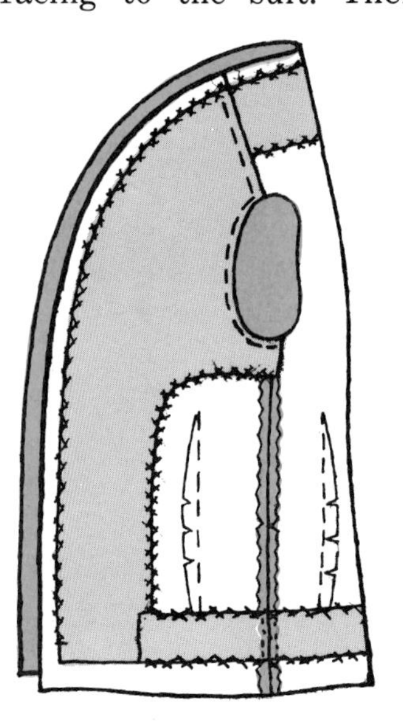

along interfacing on the suit side. Trim away seam allowances to graduated widths. Next, turn the facing to the inside, and baste all around the edge of the suit jacket to complete the step.

Be sure you bring the facing back slightly from the seamline on the inside of the suit jacket. Then press.

After you have pressed the facings, carefully pin them to the inside of the suit jacket. Use a catch-stitch to fasten them to interfacing.

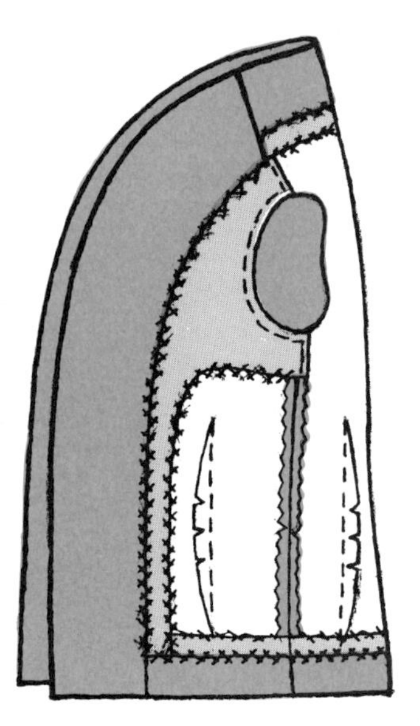

Peter Pan collar

Making this collar for a suit is similar to making one for a dress, with only a slight difference. A suit pattern provides an under and upper collar. The upper collar must be a little larger so it will roll over the under one, and collar will shape and set correctly to the neck. Cut under collar on the bias with seam at center. Join seam and press open.

Cut interfacing of hair canvas from same pattern. Sew, press seam open, stitch back seam allowances on both sides. Trim seams close to stitching.

Pin the interfacing to the wrong side of the under collar, along the center seam. Roll the collar over your index finger. Start the padding stitch from center of the collar.

Work in a circle, but inside the seam allowance lines. Work back and forth in ever-widening circle through center of collar. Fill in either side with a padding-stitch.

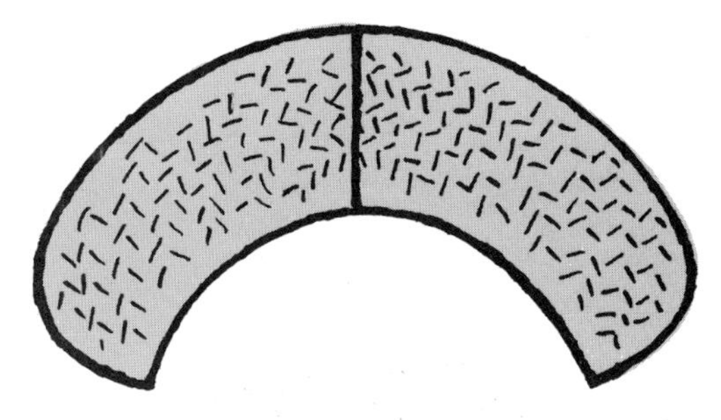

As you work, roll the collar over your finger, easing the collar as you sew. The edges of collar should curl back toward the center of the collar, if it is rolled correctly.

Trim off the interfacing seam al-

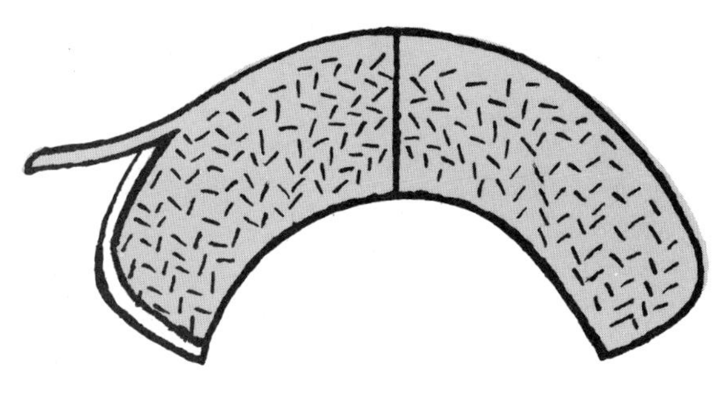

lowances all around. Pin the under collar to the upper collar, right sides together. Pin on the interfacing side. Sew all around the edge of the interfacing, easing in the upper collar a little as you pin and sew it in place. Then you can trim off the seam allowance to graduated widths.

Turn the collar right side out and baste all around, bringing the under collar in just slightly from edge.

Press the collar this way. Roll it over your hand with the right side of the collar up. Do a diagonal basting on the roll line.

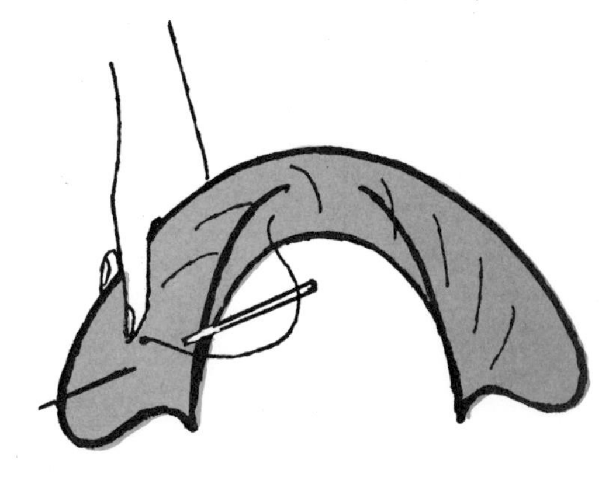

Put the collar face down on the table and roll the neck edges back, as you do for a dress collar, and pin the edges together all around the

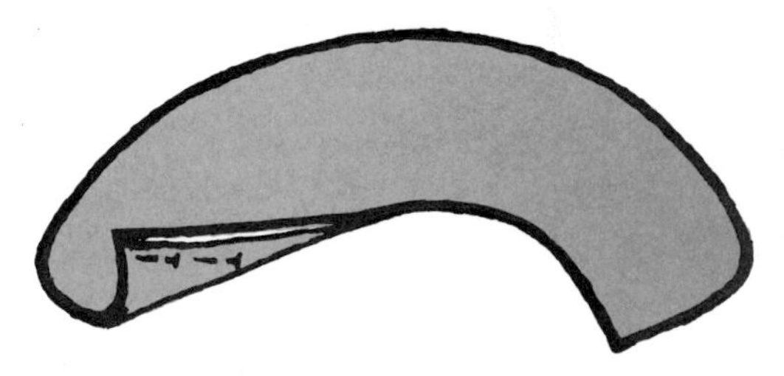

neck. The upper collar edge may be a little short of the under collar edge, but if it rolls that way, then sew it the same way. The collar is made and the roll line sewed in before it is applied to the suit. This collar can be used on a cardigan-neck suit.

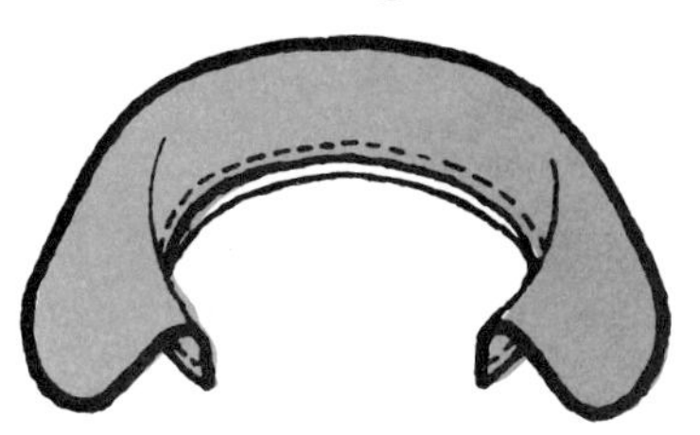

Sleeves

The sleeves can be finished just before sewing them in the jacket.

Turn the sleeve inside out. Press open the back seam allowance, using sleeve board. Next, press the front sleeve seam. As you press the seam open, clip it for the entire length. Stretch it on the length.

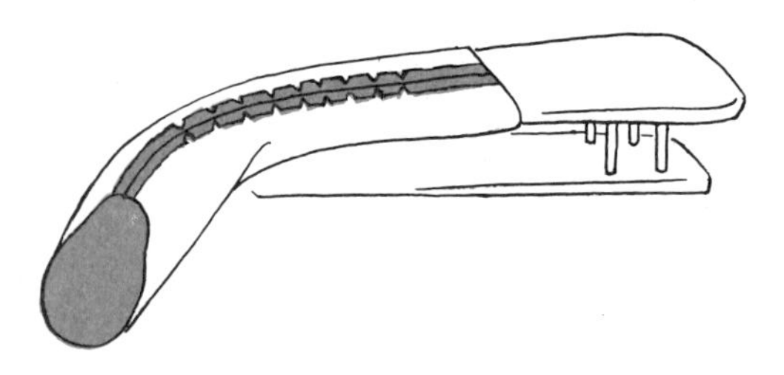

Now turn up sleeve on hem mark and press along this line. If sleeve was mounted on an underlining, baste sleeve, underlining together on hem line before turning hem.

Cut a strip of interfacing on the bias 1½ inches wider than sleeve hem. Pin one edge of the interfacing just inside the hem crease. Pin it all around the sleeve, lapping the interfacing edges at back seamline.

Pin the upper edges to the sleeve. Catch-stitch both edges to sleeve or underlining. Turn hem and catch-stitch the edge to the interfacing.

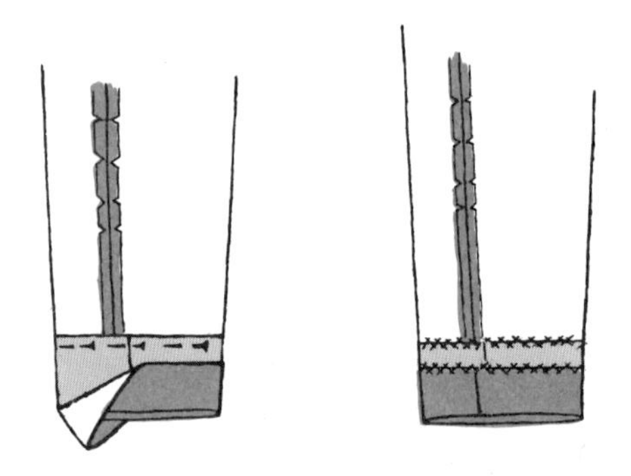

Turn the sleeve right side out. The top has been eased in to the size of the armhole. Place sleeve top over the tailor's mitt or ham and press, steaming out the fullness from the seam allowance, and shaping the cap in the top of the sleeve.

The armholes of the suit should be stay-stitched the same as the neck was before the collar was applied.

Use one strand of silk buttonhole twist. Start at the underarm of the jacket and do the same back-stitch all around armhole on the seam allowance line. Ease in the fullness at front armhole of the jacket, which gives a better fit to the bustline.

At the back of the jacket, the fullness is eased in the armhole to help

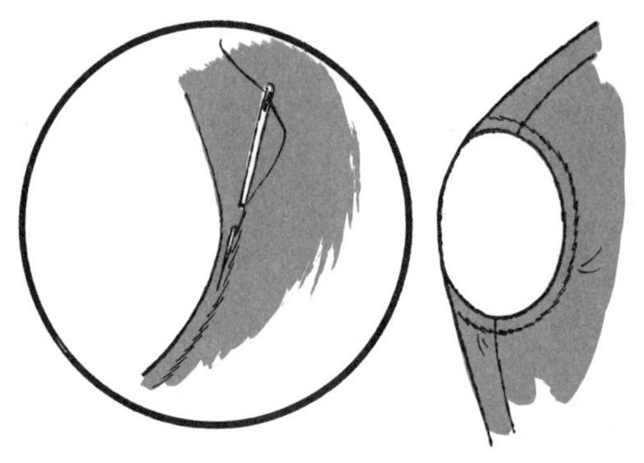

shape the back to the roundness of the shoulders. Try the jacket at this point to check armhole fit. The armhole should be eased enough to improve fit of bust and shoulder blade, but not enough to make the armhole too tight. Pin the sleeve into the suit. Be sure to match the slash marks to the top and to the underarm seams as well as to all notches. Pin on the sleeve side, with pins placed along the seam allowance line and parallel to the seam.

When you sew, start at the underarm and sew along the pin line, removing each pin as you come to it. The sleeve will go in the armhole with no difficulty. The ease won't shift when it is pinned this way, as it can do when it is basted.

Stitches

Here are instructions for making the basic stitches used in tailoring that are discussed in this book.

Running-stitch

This is the most basic stitch in sewing. It's often used for gathering, mending, tucking. Pass the needle through the fabric, taking several stitches at a time. Draw the thread through the fabric and repeat.

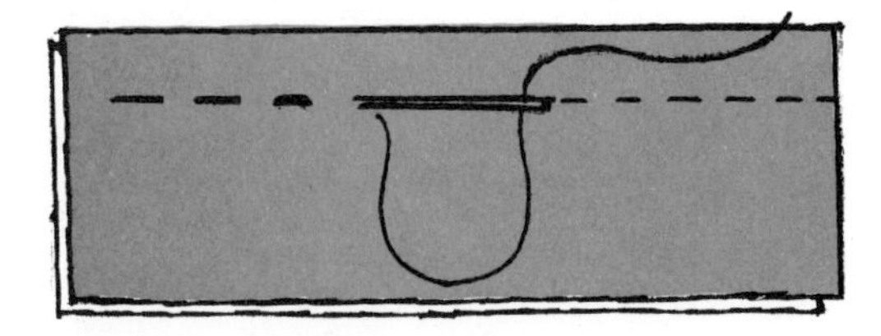

Diagonal basting

This type of basting is used to hold several layers of fabric together. Take short stitches across the fabric, forming long vertical stitches on top side. It's easier to do diagonal basting if you work backward.

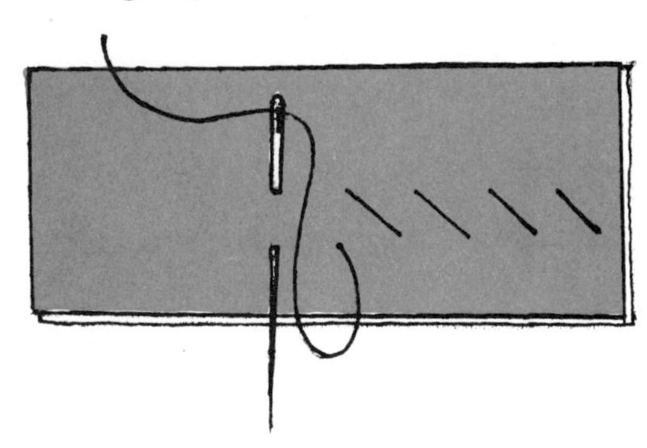

Padding-stitch

This stitch is similar to diagonal basting. The padding-stitch is used on lapels and collars to keep the interlining in place and to securely hold the roll line.

Work up and down the roll line, taking short stitches toward you. As you work back and forth, the stitch forms a herringbone design.

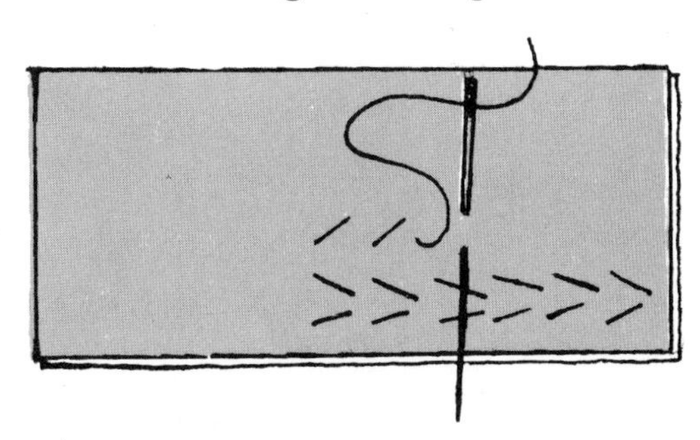

Catch-stitch

Use this stitch to finish hems on fabrics that don't fray, and to tack facings so the stitch won't hold too tightly and show on the right side.

Always work from the left to the right, taking a tiny stitch first on the hem or the facing, then on the garment. Bring the needle toward you and then back again. Keep the stitches even and loose.

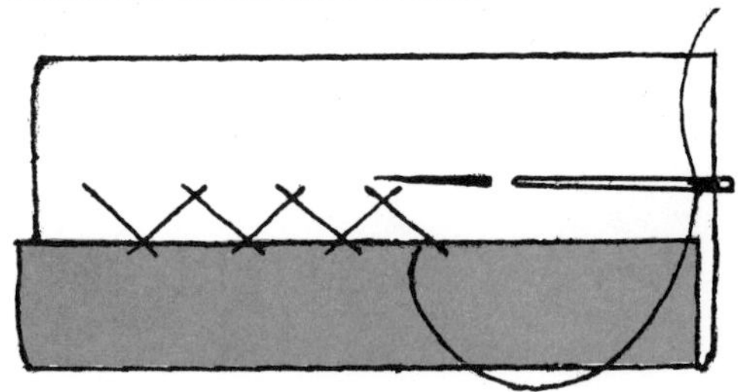

Hemming-stitch for tape

Working from right to left, catch a thread or two of the fabric of suit. Then pass the needle through edge of the tape. Make small stitches to hold the tape firmly in place.

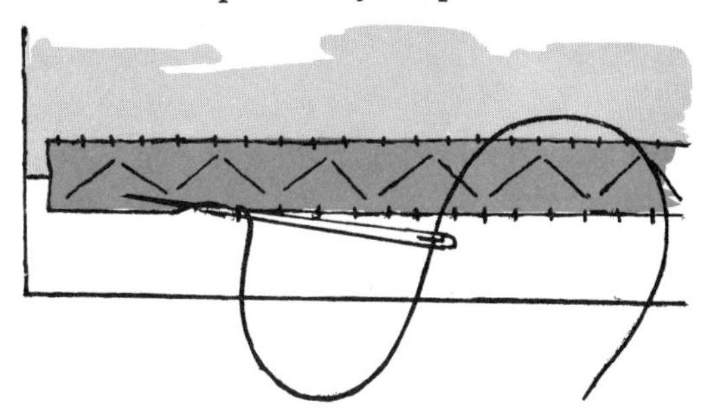

The tailored suit

The tailored suit is so named because it is often made in hard-finish fabrics, like those used by professional tailors in making men's suits.

Custom tailoring requires great skill, patience, and precision. It takes years of apprenticeship to master it. This book doesn't attempt to make a tailor of anyone. Only years of working directly with a skilled tailor can accomplish that. It does, however, illustrate a few of the points that can help a home sewer give a suit a professional look.

Many women also like to make clothes for their husbands and sons, and have made shirts, slacks, and shorts with good results. After reading this section, you may want to try a sport jacket next. Most of the tailoring techniques described here for a woman's suit are actually the same as those needed to make a man's suit. They have been simplified, but can still be applied when making a man's jacket.

Pattern companies have good patterns available that include correct sizing, fabric requirements, and instructions for making sport jackets. One of these patterns, combined with the professional tricks shown, can result in an attractive coat.

You may want to make a suit for yourself first. After you familiarize yourself with collars, sleeves, and some of the other details of tailoring, try a sport jacket. The fabrics used for them are easy to work with, generally, and do not call for such precise handling as a man's suit.

Only the finest worsteds and suitings should be used for good tailoring. Cut and assemble a tailored suit like the dressmaker suit. Do the fitting and alterations in the same way. If you have worked from a basic pattern for other garments, apply the same adjustments to the suit. Fit the jacket with enough ease to allow for interlinings and linings, and to fit over other apparel you plan to wear with the suit, such as a blouse or sweater.

Assembling the jacket

After the jacket has been fitted, it can be taken apart again by removing the bastings. While it's apart, make any alterations that are needed. Recut from adjusted pattern.

First, take the fronts of jacket and sew in basted darts. Mold and press the fronts over tailor's ham. Shape carefully at bust and hip.

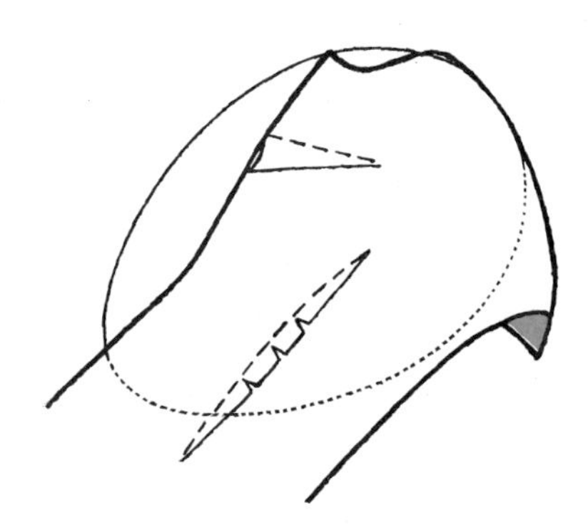

Mark for the pockets. Patch, welt, or flap pockets can be used on this type of suit. See page 50 in the section on tailoring coats for instructions on how to make all of these pockets, and variations.

When the flap pocket is made on a slant, it is important that the flap be cut correctly. Mark the position of the pocket on your jacket with a basting line. The flap for the pocket should be cut so that the top edge follows the same slant as the basting mark.

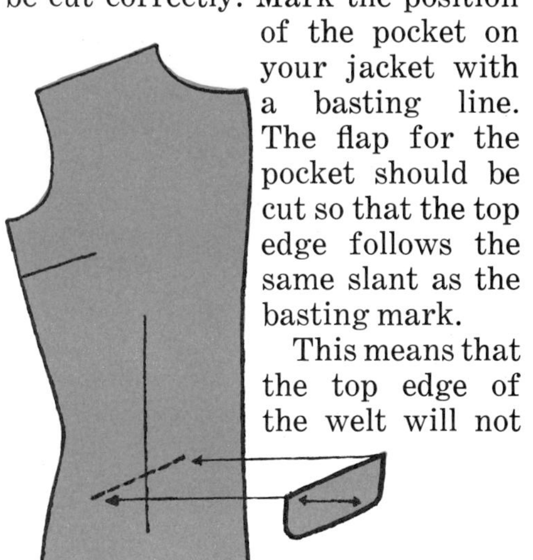

This means that the top edge of the welt will not be on straight grain of the fabric.

Cut the lining for the flap on the bias and slightly smaller than the flap. The lining should be of a firm fabric, either of a twill-type taffeta or of a heavy satin.

Pin and sew the right side of the lining to the right side of pocket flap, stretch the lining slightly to make it fit. Then trim seam, clip around the seam edges, then turn to the right side. Lining will pull in a little from the edge. This prevents any of lining from showing beyond edge of flap. To finish, baste around the flap and press.

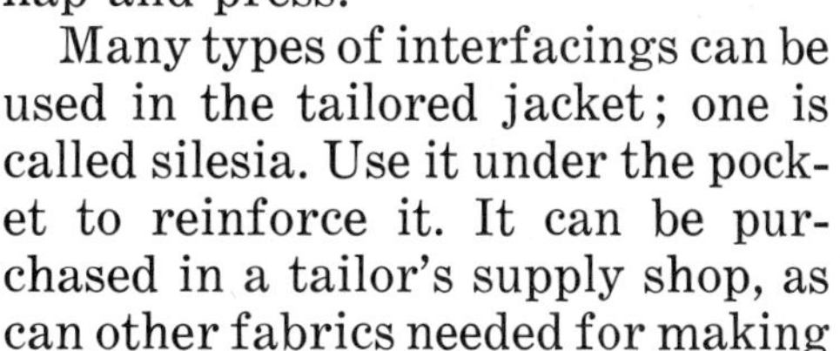

Many types of interfacings can be used in the tailored jacket; one is called silesia. Use it under the pocket to reinforce it. It can be purchased in a tailor's supply shop, as can other fabrics needed for making a suit. If silesia is not available, use a firm, commercial woven or nonwoven interfacing. Then cut interfacing about 3 inches wide and about 8 or 9 inches long, enough to extend from the side seam of suit to where the facing finishes.

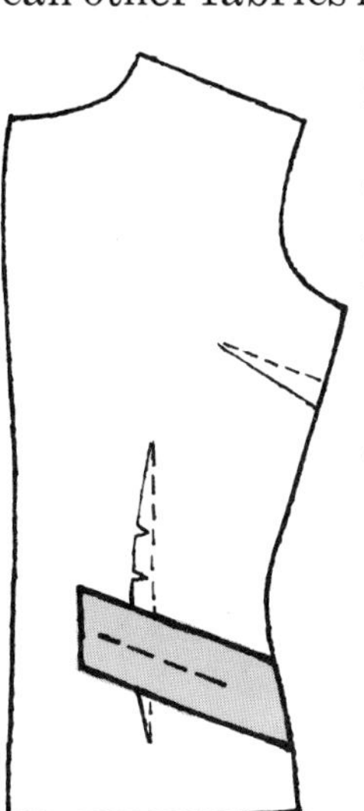

Baste it to the wrong side of the

jacket under the line of the pocket.

Cut two pocket pieces 3 inches wide and 1 inch wider than pocket flap. Cut on straight grain of suit fabric. Sew edge of flap along basting line of jacket, right side of flap to the right side of jacket. Sew one

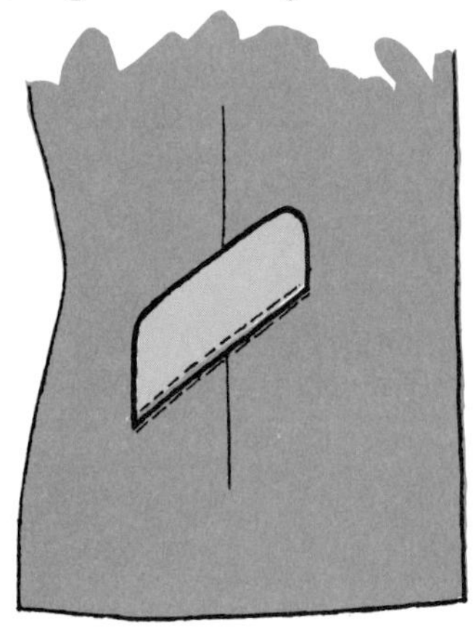

pocket piece to the under side of the flap, raw edge of pocket piece along the stitching line of the flap. When you are finished, stitching will just clear the edge of the pocket flap underneath. This stitching line will be slightly shorter at the ends than the flap stitching line.

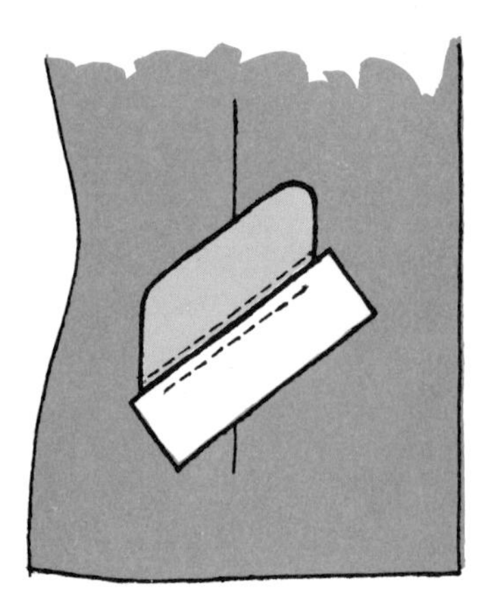

Turn to the wrong side. Stitching lines should be the same distance apart. The lower line of stitching should be slightly shorter in length than the upper line. If the lower line were made the same length, the pocket welt would show under the flap on the right side.

Slash from the center to ½ inch at either end, cut diagonally into the

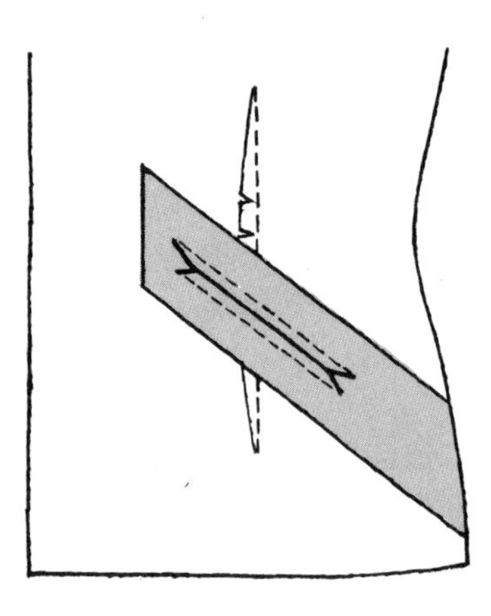

corners. Turn the under pocket piece to the inside. Fold a pleat at either end, forming a welt on the

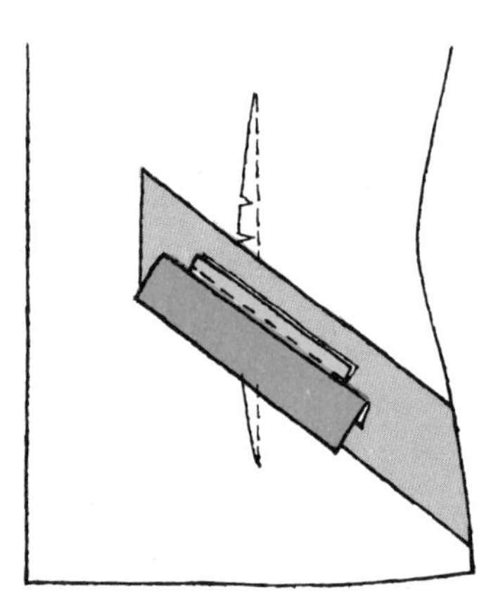

lower edge. Baste this into position

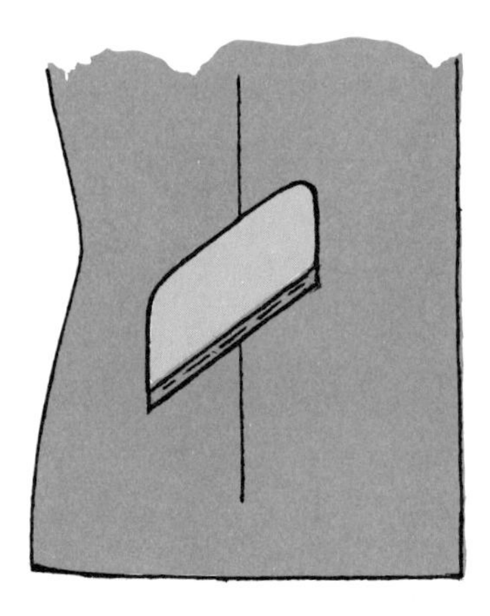

from the right side. Turn to the wrong side and fold back the under side of the jacket. Seam will show along the under-pocket piece. Stitch this to the under-pocket piece, along the original stitching line, and the lower welt is finished.

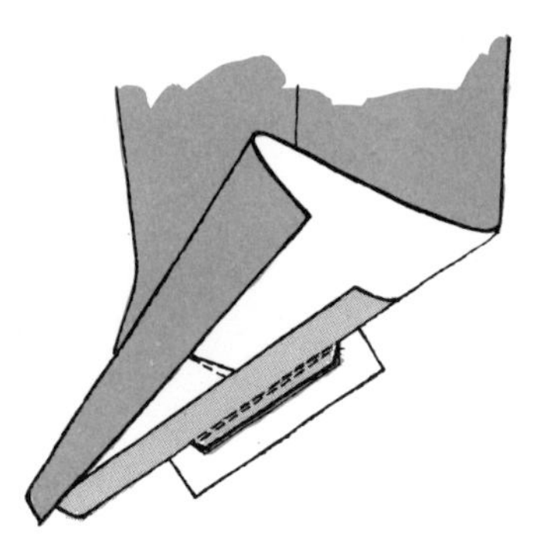

Fold the flap down on the right side; seam edge turns up on inside.

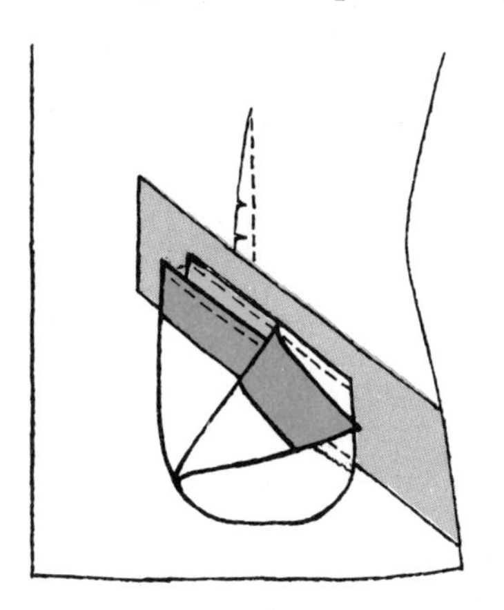

Sew the second pocket piece to this seam allowance line. Then cut lower parts of the pocket from a lining fabric. Sew them to pocket facing pieces. Turn back jacket so inside pocket shows; then stitch

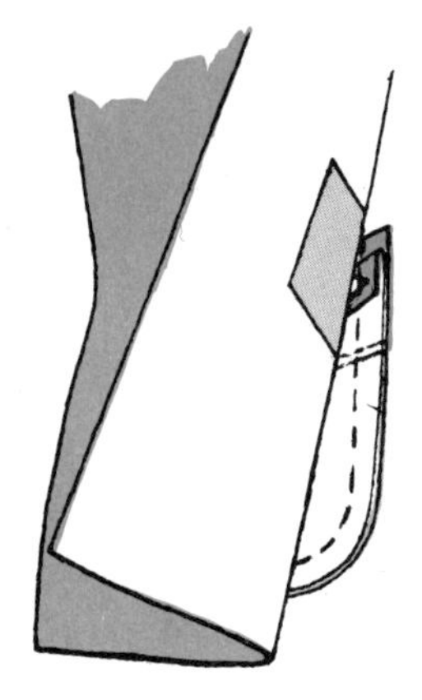

around pocket, catching points at either end in with seam. Press entire pocket over a tailor's ham so it molds and shapes to the hip.

Make the breast pocket like the ordinary welt pocket. If the welt is placed on an angle, be sure it is cut on the same angle and grain as the lower pocket flap.

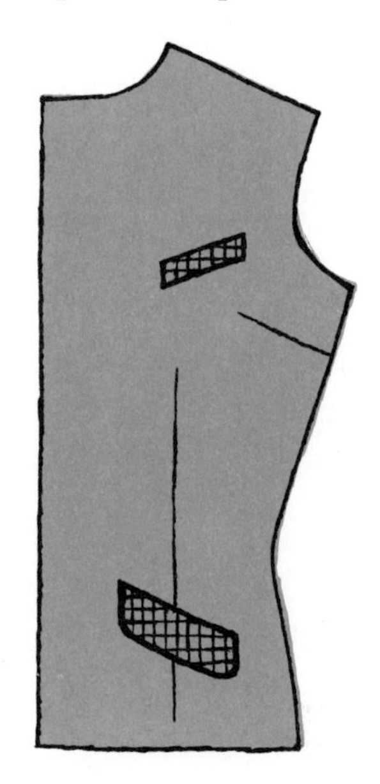

Interfacing the fronts

While the jacket is apart, interface the fronts. It is easier to shape and mold the interfacings before the jacket is assembled. Cut jacket interfacings from the pattern pieces provided. Then follow instructions on page 16, as for dressmaker suit.

Mark and sew the darts in the interfacing so that it shapes to the bust. Cut out the darts. Lap edges together over a strip of interfacing of the non-woven type; sew together. Pin interfacings to wrong side of suit front. Lay suit, right side out, over

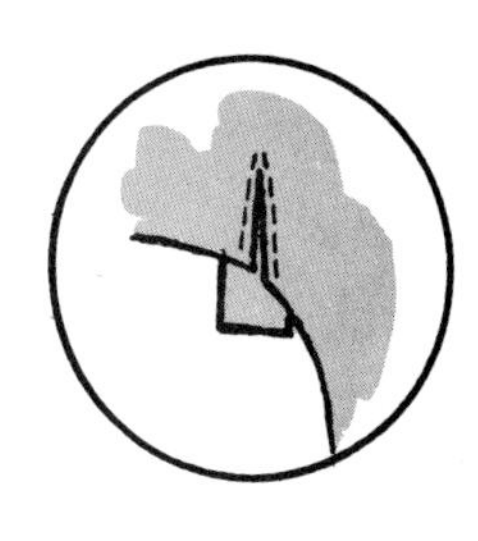

tailor's ham, baste interfacing from right side. Baste along the shoulder and around the armhole, about 2 inches in from the edge. Baste a second row of stitching from the center of the shoulder down to the end of the interfacing, about 2 inches in from the first stitching. Baste down from the edge of the neck to the lower edge of the interfacing, about 3 inches in from the front edge.

Baste along the curve of the interfacing under the bust. Finally, baste the front edges together up to the roll line, along the roll line to the neck. As a rule, this line is not indicated on the pattern.

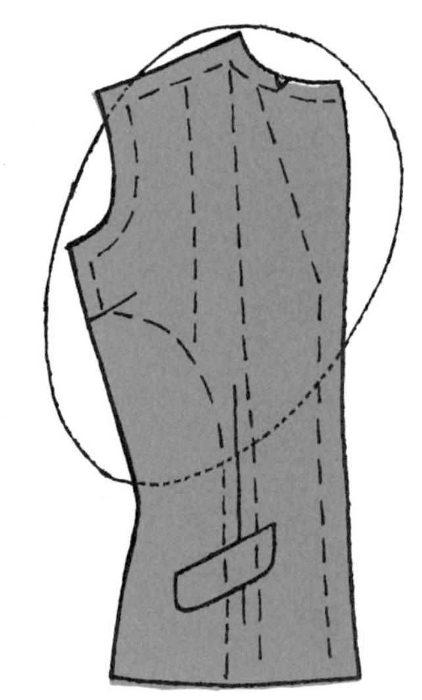

It may be necessary to pin the collar on and try the suit to find the accurate roll line; usually, it is from the top buttonhole to a point where lapel rolls into the collar. Put a row of pins to mark line. Remove jacket, run basting thread to mark.

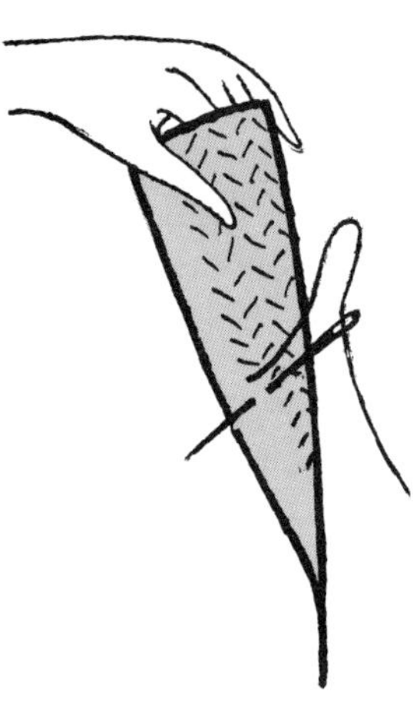

Starting at the roll line, begin padding the interfacing to the lapel, and rolling it over your hand as you work. Stitch it, back and forth, as you fill in the entire lapel, except for the seam allowance at neck and front edges. Do this on both

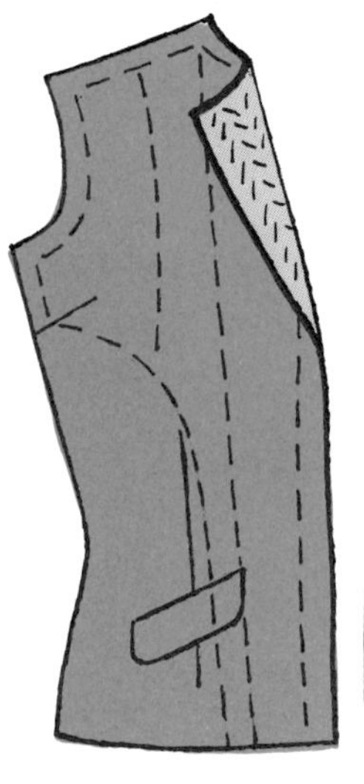

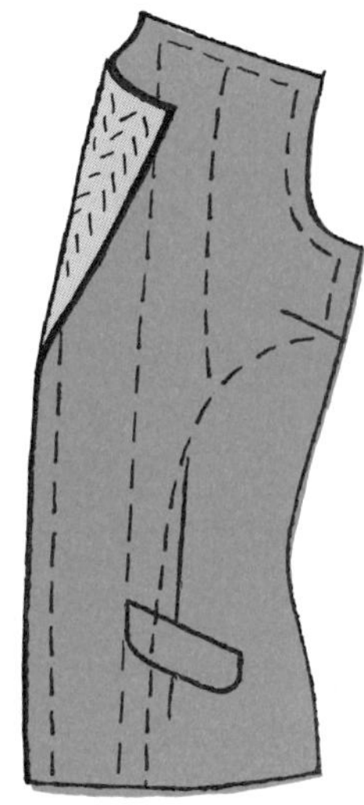

the jacket fronts. Trim away the interfacing, leaving about a $\frac{3}{4}$ inch seam allowance on the jacket edge, rather than the usual $\frac{5}{8}$ inch.

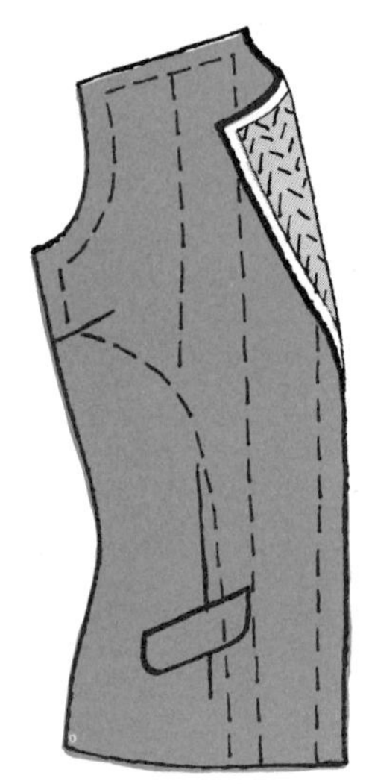

Tape the front edge of the suit jacket to prevent stretching and to give a firm edge. (See page 19 for directions.) You can also use tape along roll line of lapel. Pin, baste, and sew it to lapel in the same way.

Joining and pressing

Join the side seams and any back seam of the jacket. Use a straight inside seam. The shoulder seams must be given special handling.

There is always a dart in the back shoulder of the woman's jacket pattern to take care of the normal back fullness. This dart is put in the pattern on all women's suits, regardless of the style.

If the figure is round-shouldered, this dart should be made even deeper than indicated to make allowances for the extra fitting needed.

If you plan to make your suit of worsted, or any fabric that can be eased, eliminate the dart, then cut the shoulder seam in a straight line, rather than following the shaping of the back dart.

When you sew the two seams, pin the edges together on the front shoulder side. Space the back fullness evenly, and pin. The fullness

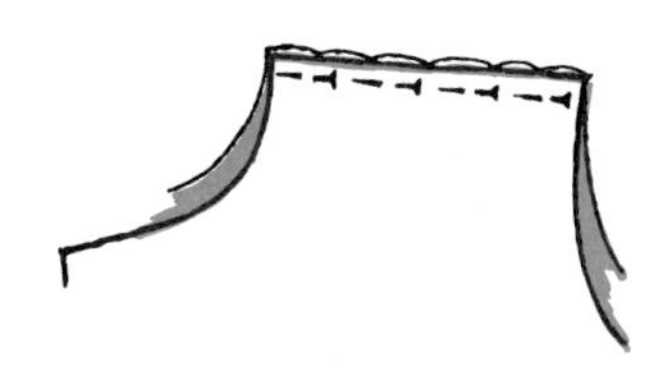

can be eased in better, if you sew with the back on the lower side toward the sewing machine.

The teeth of the under carriage take the under layer of fabric through faster, and the fullness is eased in with no difficulty.

Stretch the front shoulder seam slightly as you sew to be sure that the fullness will all be eased in correctly and smoothly.

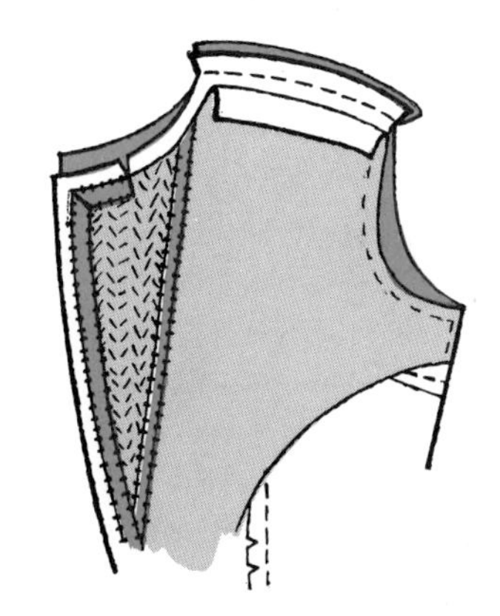

Pressing the suit

As the dressmaker suit, the first pressing is the most important; do all pressing over a tailor's ham.

Turn the jacket inside out. First, press the shoulder seam. Put the jacket over the ham so the front shoulder is toward the center of the ham, and the back shoulder curves around the wide part of the ham and over the curved edge.

Press the seam open, stretching the back seam and letting the front seam curve. Turn your jacket right side out and hang it over your hand to check the shape of the shoulder. It should follow the curve of the hand, with the back rounded and the front shoulder concave and shaping in toward the palm. When sewed and pressed this way, the jacket will follow the curve of your shoulders, and not look as though the sleeves were pulling toward the back.

Now press the rest of the jacket over the ham, molding the hip and chest at the wide part of the ham. Press the waistline toward the narrow part of the ham.

Press all darts toward the front. Sometimes the curve of the dart must be clipped so that the suit can be pressed flat. At the waistline, the side and the back seams must also be clipped. Now press open the seams in the suit to finish it.

Collar

An under collar is cut in two pieces on the bias for the tailored suit. It is made of a hard flannel. You can buy it already cut at a tailor's supply shop in a color to match your suit. Otherwise, get a piece of firm flannel in worsted and cut your own from the under collar pattern. Or, if the suit fabric is not too heavy, cut the collar from the same fabric.

Sew up the center seam of the under collar and press it open. The interfacing can be cut in hair canvas, although on a tailored suit, heavy Belgian linen will generally make a firmer collar. Cut the linen interfacing from the under collar pattern. Trim off the center seam allowance. Lap together over a piece of tape, and stitch back and forth across the tape, holding the two edges together. If you have a zigzag machine, you can sew with it.

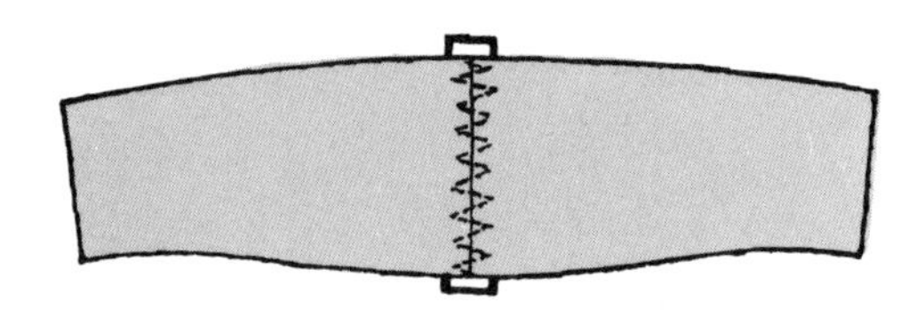

Trim off ¾ inch at sides and top edge of the under collar. Lay the interfacing against the wrong side of the under collar and start padding and rolling the collar over your hand. The interfacing will be even with the neck edge, but larger than the rest of the under collar as you start the padding-stitch. Work the same as on dressmaker suit collar.

Then trim off inside neck edges of the under collar at the seam allowance line. Fold the under collar on the roll line and press lightly. Now the collar is ready to be applied to the neck. Never tape the neck of a quality suit to prevent stretching. Instead, stay-stitch by hand with a silk buttonhole twist. Start at the center front of the neck or at the point where the collar starts.

Bring needle through to the right side on the seam allowance line. Take a back-stitch for ½ inch and bring it forward ¼ inch on the neck side of the thread. Continue this way all around the neckline. The

neck can be eased on this thread if it's stretched at all. There is an elasticity to the stitch that holds but doesn't hold too rigidly.

The top of the lapel should be notched at the point where the front ends of the collar join. Lap the under collar over the right side of the neckline, just covering stay-stitch around the neck. Pin the collar at the back, the shoulder seams, and the front edge at the notch. Sew to neck with a small hemming-stitch.

Baste the roll line on the collar and the lapel. Put the lapel and collar on a tailor's ham and lightly press in the roll line on your suit.

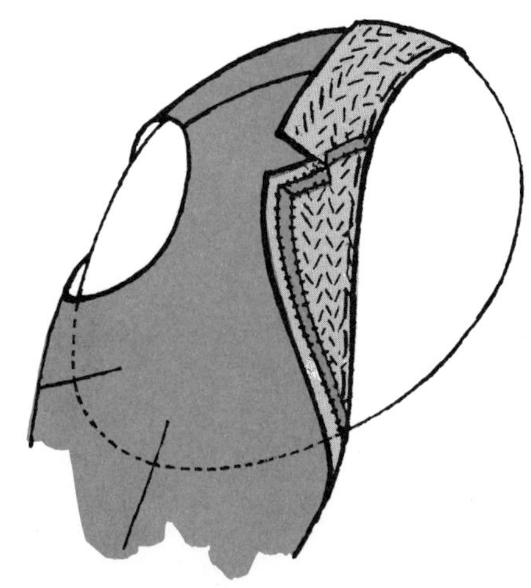

Applying facings

Mark for notches and shoulder seam on the upper collar with clip mark. Also mark the center back of neck with a clip mark. Pin the collar to the facings from the shoulder seam mark around the front of the collar. Pin the seam allowance line of the front of the collar at the point where the front collar joins the facings. Sew the collar to the facings on the seam allowance line. Clip in to the stitching line on the front where the collar joins. Next, clip the seam all around the neck of the suit and then press open the seam.

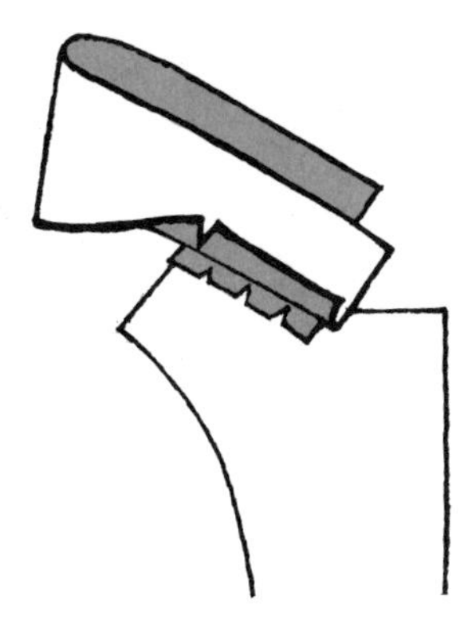

Place the jacket right side up on a tailor's ham. Place the facing in position on the right side of the jacket. Baste the facing so that the ease is allowed for the correct roll of the lapel. The first basting is from the point of the lapel toward the inside edge of the facing. Ease in the facing as you baste it. Let the lapel roll over the curve of the tailor's ham as you baste.

Next, baste along the top of the lapel. Again, ease the facing and let it roll over the curve of the ham as you baste it in place.

Now ease the front of the lapel to the end of the roll line. Place the lapel on the ham so that it rolls over the curve of the ham in the direction that you're basting, to allow ease. The remainder of the facing is basted into place along the inside and the lower edge. At these points, it

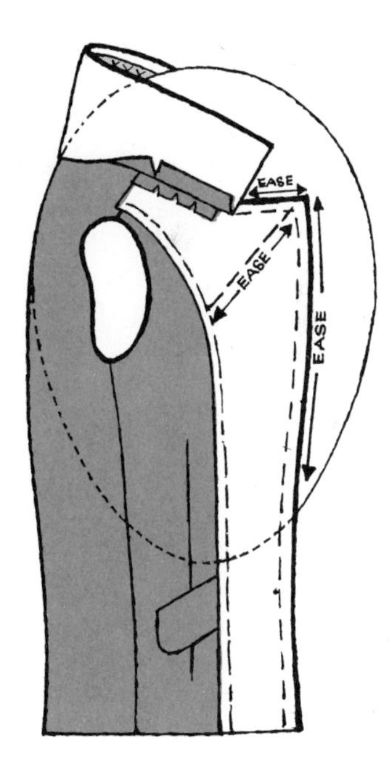

is not necessary to allow ease. Turn the suit to the inside and stitch the facing from the bottom of the jacket to the point where the collar joins the neck. Be sure to ease it in at the edge and top of the suit lapel where you basted it.

Trim the seam allowance to graduated widths before turning the facing to the inside. Trim the seam on

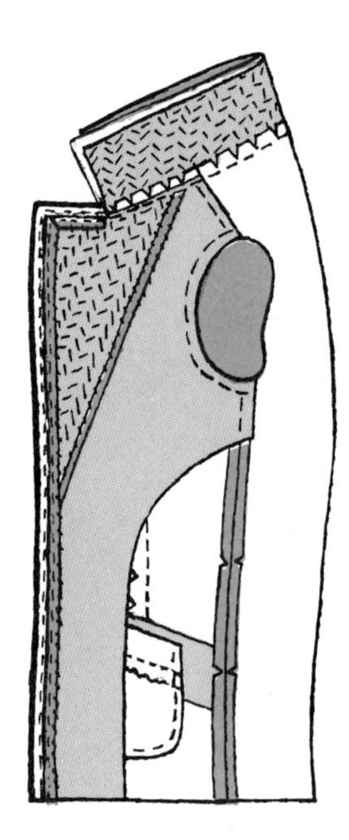

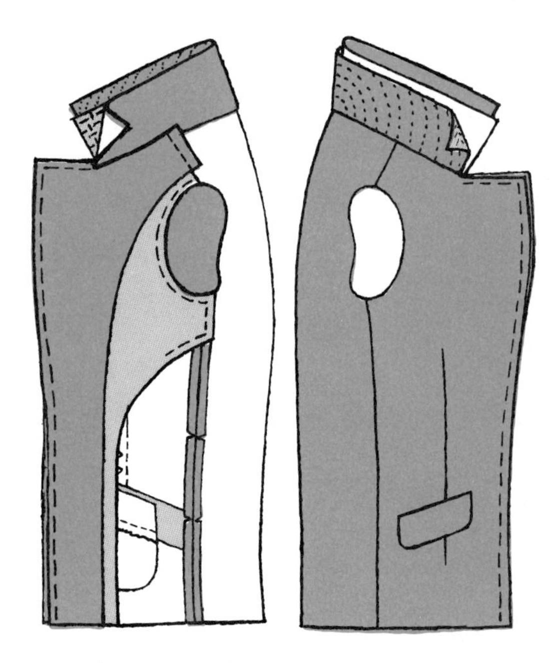

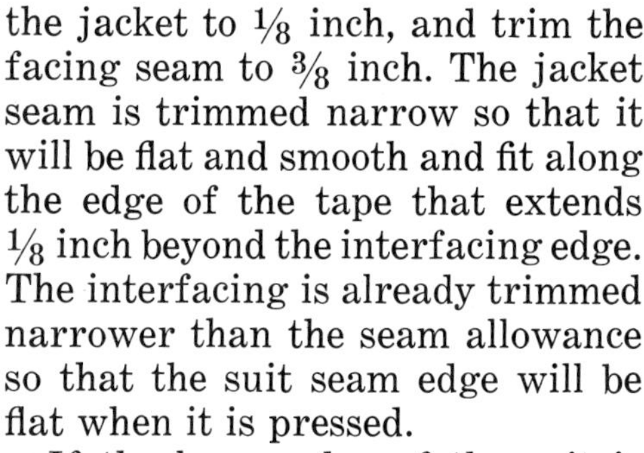

the jacket to 1/8 inch, and trim the facing seam to 3/8 inch. The jacket seam is trimmed narrow so that it will be flat and smooth and fit along the edge of the tape that extends 1/8 inch beyond the interfacing edge. The interfacing is already trimmed narrower than the seam allowance so that the suit seam edge will be flat when it is pressed.

If the lower edge of the suit is curved, clip into the stitching line all around the curved seam before you turn the facing to the inside.

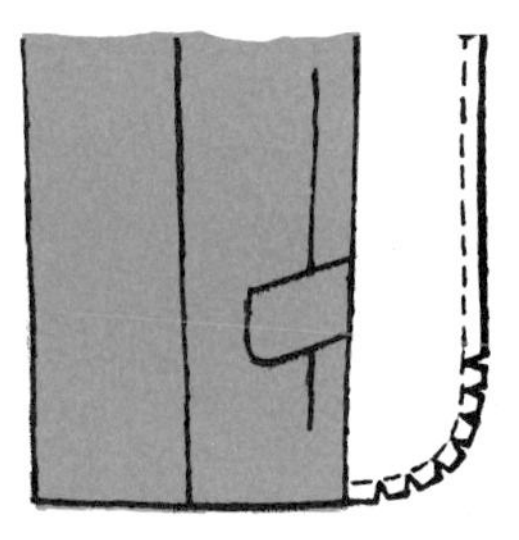

Carefully baste the edge of the facing. Bring it in slightly toward the inside of the jacket at the lower end. At the lapel, bring the jacket edge in slightly. Press the lower edge of the jacket on the inside. At lapel and collar, press on the jacket side.

Put the jacket right side down on a tailor's ham, and smooth back facing to the inside on lower part of jacket. Pin in place. Roll the lapel to the right side, smooth back the upper facing to the inside and pin

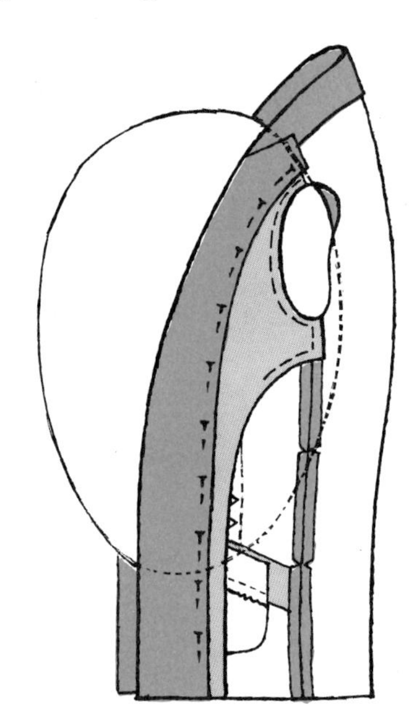

it in place. The lapel is rolled as it will be worn. It's pinned so the ease allowed for the perfect rolling of the jacket lapel will not be smoothed back into the suit and tacked the wrong way, which would spoil the roll line of the suit. Run a stitching line along the seam allowance line that is on the outside edge of the upper collar. This stitching line will act as a guide for trimming, and also for correct shaping of upper collar.

Turn under the edges of the upper collar on the seam allowance line. Shape it carefully as you turn it under, since this will be the finished collar edge. Press it carefully all around and then trim the seam to 3/8 inch. It may be necessary to clip to the seam allowance line at certain points as you turn it so that it can be shaped later.

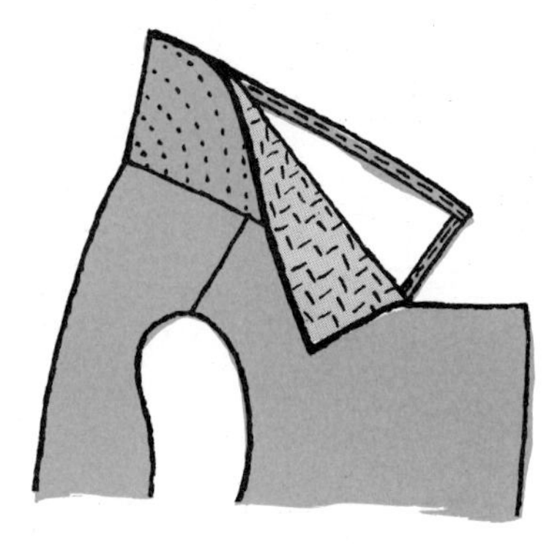

Pin the under collar 1/16 inch in from the edge of the upper collar. Ease the upper collar slightly to fit and to create a better roll. Sew the raw edge of the under collar to the upper collar with a fine hemmingstitch. Roll the collar to the right

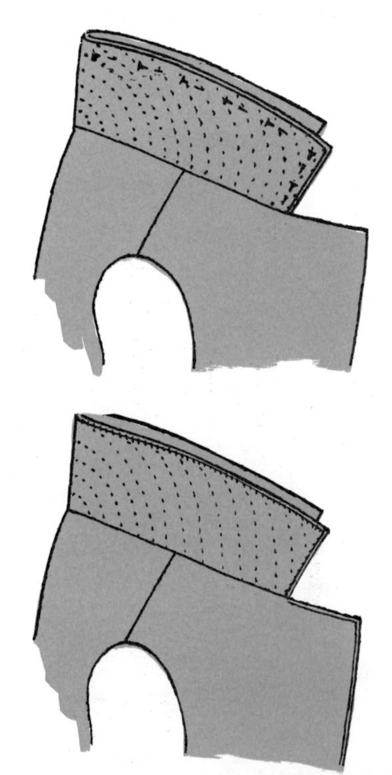

side as it will be worn, and pin and then tack the loose edge of the upper collar to the back neck. The collar

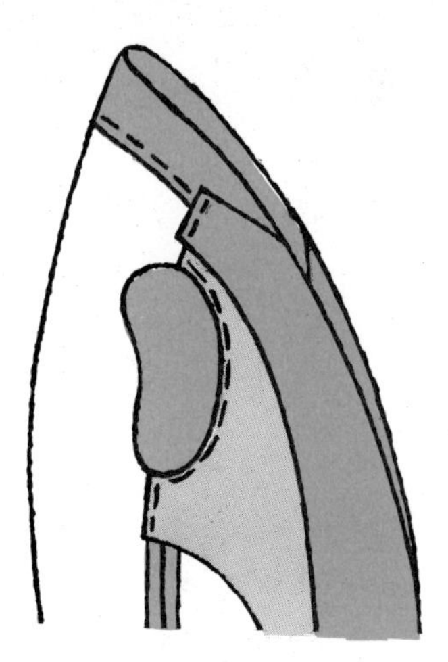

should roll correctly with no "dog-eared" corners because it was eased properly before the facings and under collar were sewed. In the final pressing of the jacket, the roll line crease will be pressed out. The collar and lapel are shaped to roll softly on their own roll line.

The inside facing can then be

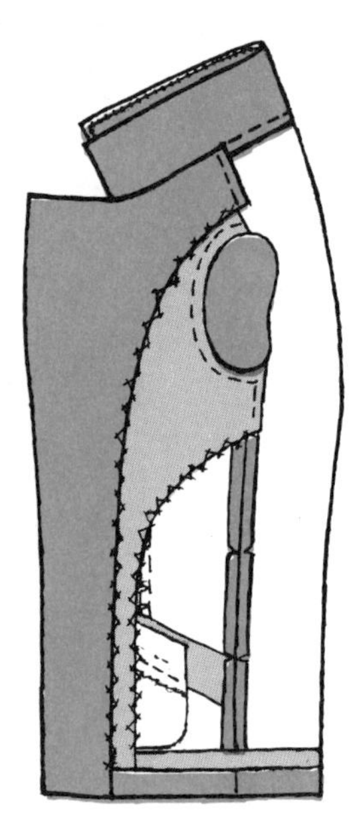

catch-stitched to the interfacing of jacket. The hem of the jacket can be turned up, then pressed on the hemline. It'll have an interfacing to give a firm line to the edge of suit.

Cut a strip of hair canvas or of woven interfacing on the bias. Make it about 2 inches wider than hem. Fold the interfacing back 1 inch and then press. Tack the fold line of the interfacing to the fold line of the hem with a blind tacking stitch that doesn't show on right side. Catch-stitch

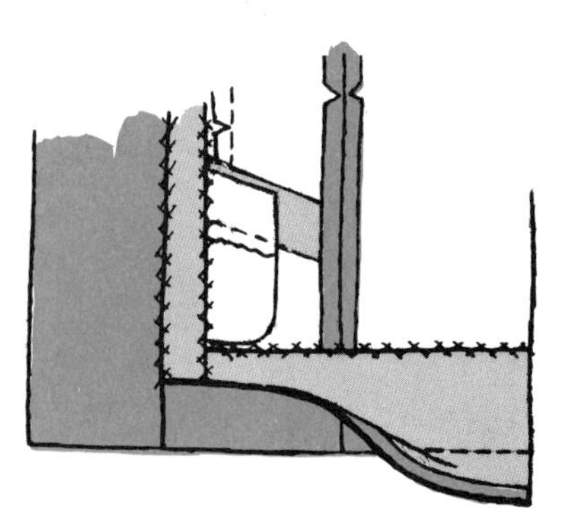

the upper edge of interfacing to the jacket. Pick up only a thread of the jacket so the stitching won't show on the outside. If jacket was mounted, catch to underlining. Catch-stitch the hem to the interfacing.

Lining the jacket

The tailored jacket is lined in much the same manner as a coat is lined, with the exception of the sleeves. See page 55 for lining instructions.

Sleeves

The tailored suit always has a two-piece sleeve. Sew up the front seam of the sleeve. Clip along the seam, and then press it open, stretching it slightly as you press.

Cut a piece of silesia about 6 inches wide on the bias. If silesia is not available, use hair canvas. Mark the hemline on the sleeve. Mark ½ inch in on the lower edge of the silesia. Baste it to the hemline along the ½-inch mark. Turn back

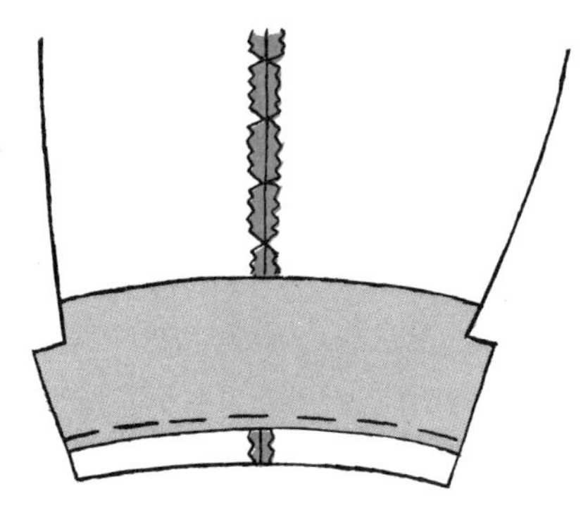

the hem on sleeve, press and shape the silesia inside the hem. Catch-

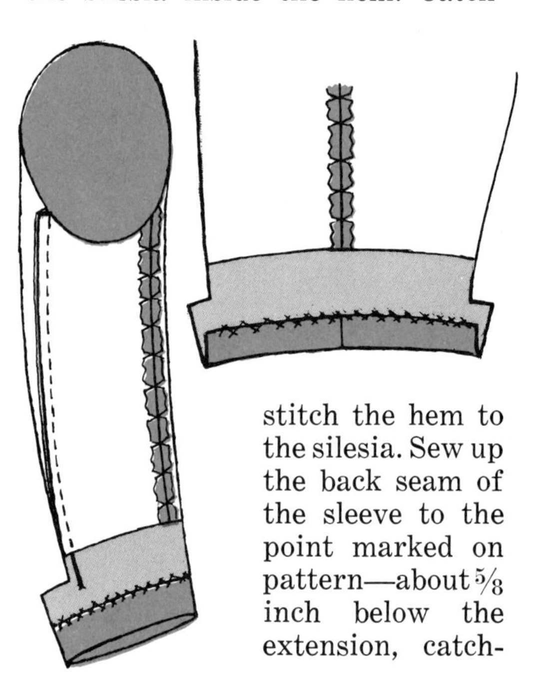

stitch the hem to the silesia. Sew up the back seam of the sleeve to the point marked on pattern—about ⅝ inch below the extension, catching the silesia in the seam. Clip into the seamline on the under sleeve side. Baste the rest of the lower sleeve closed. Press the back sleeve seam open. Press the extension toward front sleeve, and then catchstitch the underlap of the extension to the silesia. The loose ends of the hem are catch-stitched to the inside hem of the suit sleeve.

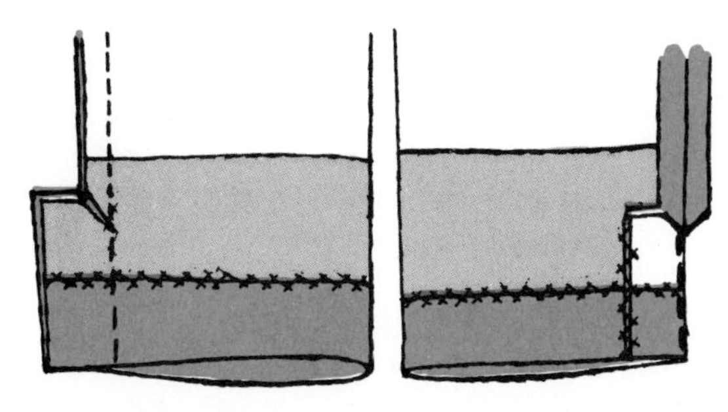

Measure over ½ inch from the basting line, holding the sleeve end closed and do a stay-stitch, as was used to stay the neck. Catch all the thicknesses of the opening, except the top layer of the sleeve. Sew up sleeve lining and press the seams

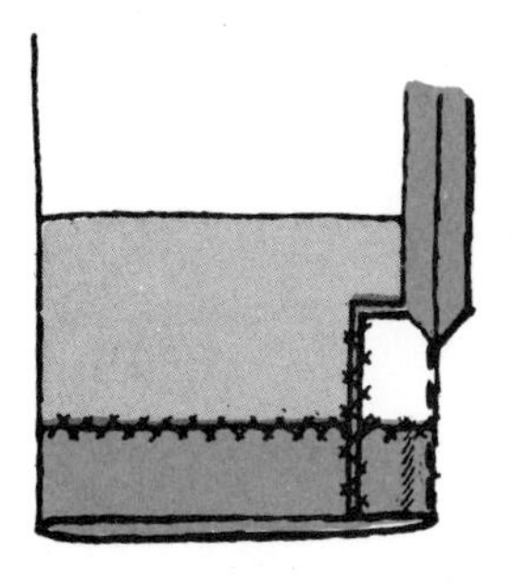

open. Then turn lining and the sleeves inside out. Lap suit lining seams over the sleeve seams and then tack together—leaving them free for about 3 inches from lower and upper ends of the sleeve.

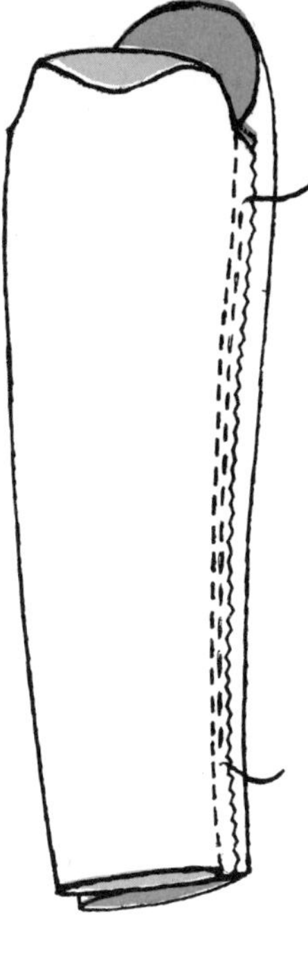

Turn the sleeve so the suit sleeve is inside lining. Turn under the loose edge of the lining at the lower end of the sleeve and slip-stitch it to the edge of the sleeve hem.

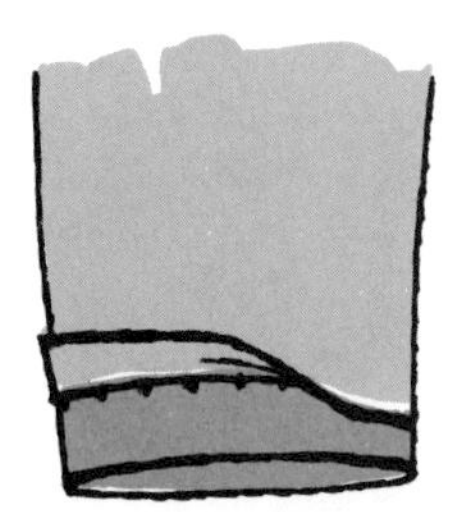

Now the sleeve is ready to be sewed into the jacket, as you do for the Dressmaker Suit (see instructions on page 32).

A tailored suit usually has a little roll to the top of the sleeve that gives it a smoother shoulder line. This is created with a small padding strip. Cut a piece of sheet cotton 8 inches long, and 2 inches wide. Fold it in half and baste to the top of sleeve on the sleeve side. Baste center of the strip to the seamline of the sleeve. You will find that the armhole seam turns toward the sleeve; this puts the padding strip between the sleeve and the armhole seam, forming a smooth top to the shoulder. For a woman with extremely sloping or narrow shoulders, a small pad will improve looks of this suit. Buy it at a tailor's supply shop, or make it from graduated layers of sheet cotton, cut and shaped to fit. Pin and tack pads to jacket interfacing and armhole seam. Pad should extend into seam for ⅜ inch.

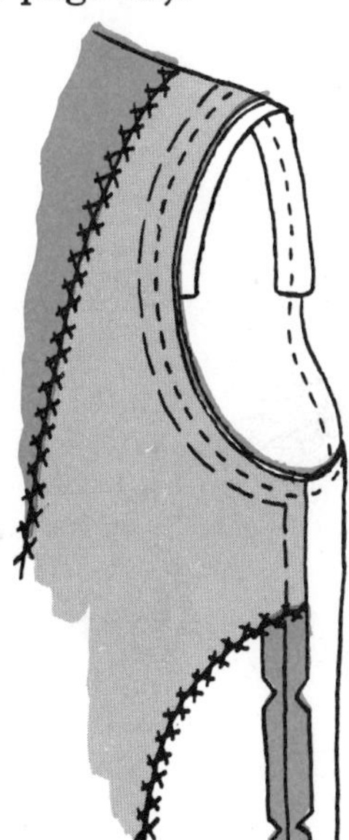

Tailoring coats

Statistics show that women make fewer coats than any other garment type. This is surprising, since many coats are easy to make. Few pattern pieces are needed for the average coat. This makes them easier to sew.

Of course, there are complicated styles that are difficult to make. The notched-collar coat does call for an experienced sewer, when it's made in a heavy fabric. Many home sewers visualize *all* coats in heavy tweed or woolen fabrics that are hard to sew. Actually, coats are made from all types of fabrics—from chiffon to the heaviest wool fleece.

Instead of beginning with the difficult notched-collar coat, consider making a straight box coat or a flared coat with a cardigan neck. There is no collar to make and very little fitting to do. Make it in a medium-weight tweed; this fabric does not show mistakes, is easy to sew.

Next, you might try a glamorous evening coat in satin or brocade, with a deep Peter Pan collar, or a large scarf collar. After that, you will be ready to make a basic black coat, perhaps in a more fitted style, and with a fashionable stand-away neckline. Build your tailoring skill gradually, and you'll find it satisfying, as well as economical.

Most of the methods used in making the dressmaker suit also apply to a coat. If you examine it closely, you will find that a coat is really an elongated version of your suit jacket. Often, when you can't find a coat pattern in the style you want, it's possible to take a jacket that has the style detail you like, and simply cut it longer. It is a good idea, however, to get the jacket pattern in the next size larger, so that the coat will have plenty of ease to be worn over dresses and suits. You can make an unlined coat in a lightweight fabric in the same pattern size as your suit.

Don't let this information confuse you when you buy a new pattern.

Adjusting coats

When you buy a coat pattern, always get the same size you wear in a dress or suit. The pattern allows enough ease to fit over other garments and for the lining. The same fitting alterations made in other garments also apply to the coat. If you haven't yet made a basic pattern for yourself, do it before you cut your coat. See the Creative Sewing Book on *Pattern Adjustments* for instructions on how to make a basic pattern.

There are two important fitting points to check—the hang in front and back. If you have altered your pattern first from a basic pattern, the fit should be correct.

Very full bust

Even though the coat fits around the figure, the very full bust will affect the way the coat hangs.

With this figure problem, the coat appears to ride up in front and hang low in back (A). A simple alteration shown on the basic pattern will solve the problem. Slash through the coat pattern across the front, and add to length (B). If you don't need to lengthen front, you'll definitely have to shorten the back. Add either the amount you lengthen the front or the amount you shorten the back to the front dart. Take up the side bust dart this extra amount, and the coat will hang correctly. This adjustment is used for a loose-style coat. On a fitted coat, make adjustments in same amount at same points as on basic.

B

A

Round-shouldered figure

The figure curves forward, causing the coat to droop in the front and hang open. Round shoulders cause the coat to ride up in the back, and protrude at the center (A).

The alteration for this fault will also show on your basic, so correct the pattern before you cut the coat.

With this figure problem, chest is hollow and front shoulders are narrow. Shorten front with a dart under the neck, and narrow the front shoulders as shown on the basic pattern (B).

At the back, open pattern under neck to give more length for rounded back. Make deeper back dart, which shapes coat to rounded back and narrows top back shoulders, so front seams and back shoulder seams are same length.

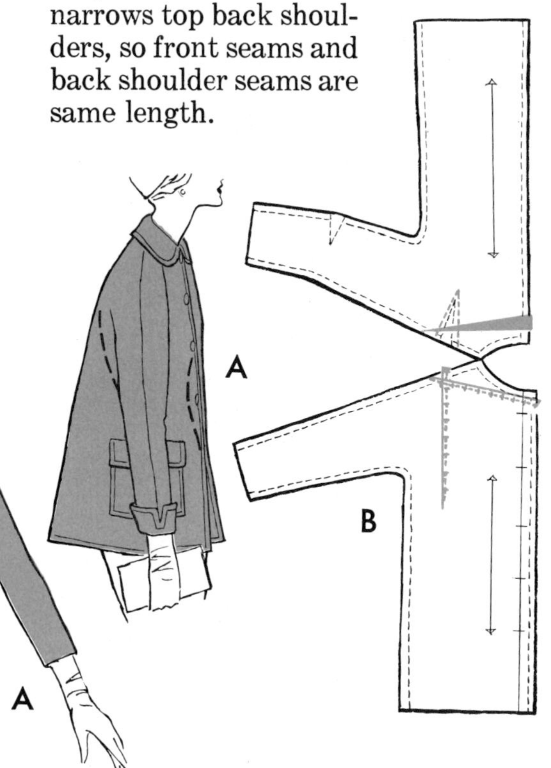

Assembling the coat

Unlined coat

If possible, cut the seams slightly wider on lighter-weight fabrics. Cut out, mark, and sew up the coat just as you do for dresses and suits.

Baste in the sleeves and try on the coat. Then mark any additional fitting that's needed on it.

Finish all seams before sleeves or facings are sewed to the coat. Do this as you sew up the coat. Simply turn back the seams on each edge by

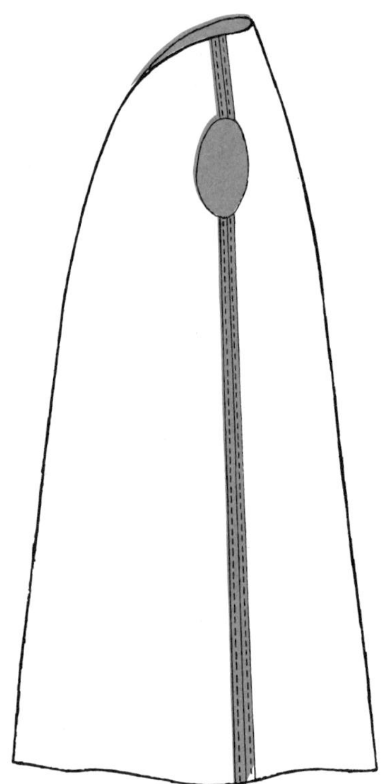

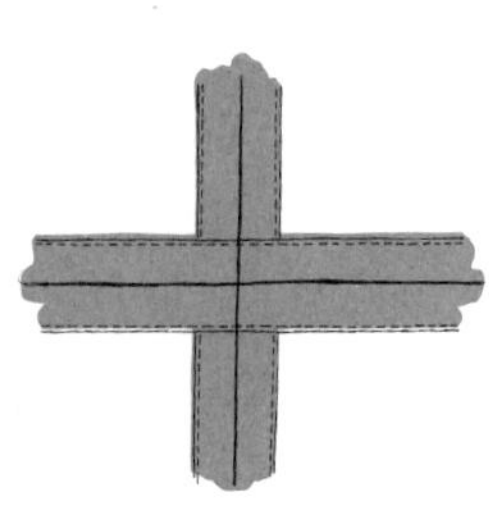

machine. Be careful never to sew a seam across another one, unless the first seam is completely finished. If seams are not wide enough so you can turn back, bind the edges with seam binding. Either bind armhole seams, or turn in, whip seam edges by hand.

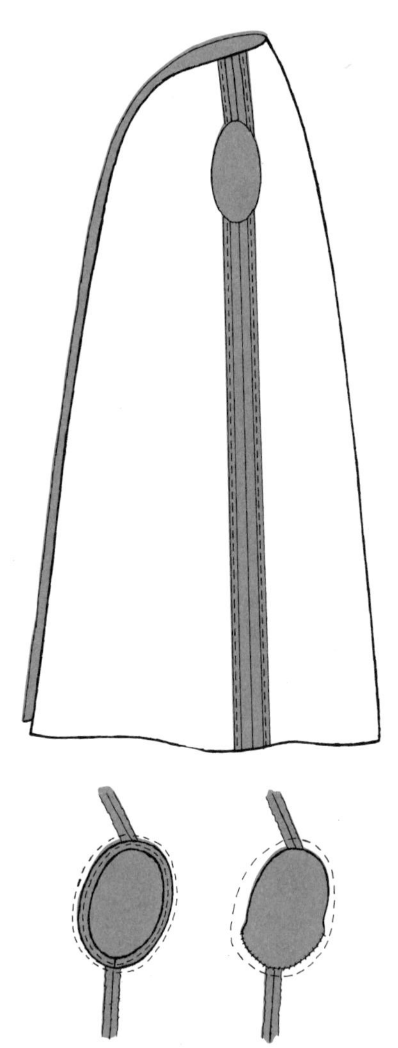

Coats that are washable can be interfaced with nonwoven interfacing or a commercial woven interfacing. Or, you may prefer to use organdy or lawn that has been preshrunk. Sew the interfacing to the facing before applying it to the coat.

If there are buttonholes, make them first. Use a piece of nonwoven interfacing under each one to prevent any raveling at buttonholes.

If the coat has a collar, make it as for a dress. (See sections on collars on page 21, and in Creative Sewing Book on *Professional Sewing Tips.*)

Cut the interfacing from the same pattern as the facing. Be sure interfacing is preshrunk. Pin and stitch it all around the facing, close to the seam edge. Bind the inside edge of the facing, as you did the seams, or cut away the interfacing on the inside edge for 1/4 inch. Turn this edge back and stitch it.

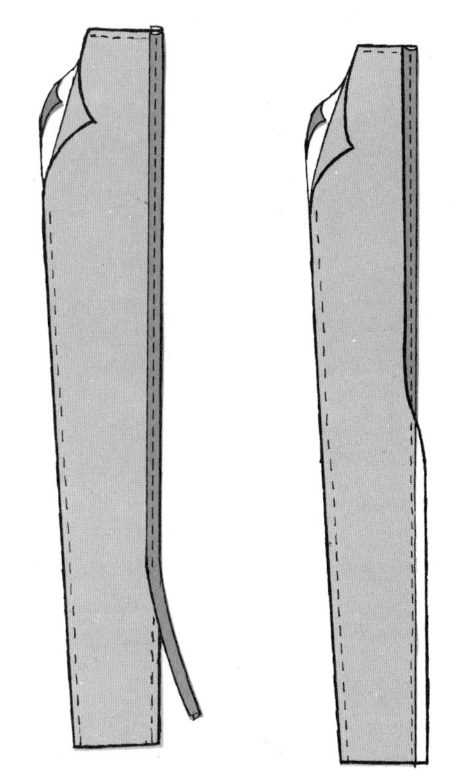

Apply the coat facing in the same way that you would for a dress. Then turn the hem of the coat, trim it, and press. Sew seam binding to the hem edge and stitch hem in place.

Evening coats

These coats should be cut in fabrics made to look crisp and elegant. Cut out the coat and then cut an underlining of preshrunk fabric from the same pattern pieces.

Remove the pattern from the cutout pieces after marking darts, tucks, and other details on the underlining. Then put the wrong side of the coat against the unmarked side of the underlining. Press the two layers together and then pin all around the edges. Sew two layers, just outside seam allowance line.

After it is mounted, sew up the coat and try it on for a fitting. If there are alterations needed, correct the pattern and recut from it.

The evening coat does not require the interfacing of hair canvas, generally used for suits and coats. If the coat has a cardigan neck or a set-on collar, like the Peter Pan collar, interface it with nonwoven interfacing, or a commercial woven one. These are lightweight, but have good body. It's important that the color of the interfacing does not show through the upper fabric. Hair canvas, available in beige or gray, sometimes shows a shadow when used under light-colored silks, while the lighter-weight interfacings do not show through.

When the coat has a rolled lapel, use a woven interfacing. When the roll is on the bias grain, it gives a softer line than if a nonwoven interfacing is used.

Facings, buttonholes, and collars can all be finished the same way as on the dressmaker suit. Lining a coat is illustrated on page 55.

Wool coats

The coat does not need to be mounted, if you use a very heavy, firm fabric. Otherwise, use the same type of underlining as for an evening coat. Make collars, facings, and buttonholes as for the dressmaker suit.

Pockets

Many pockets serve as a design detail, as well as being functional.

The inside patch pocket with a flap, or the regular patch pocket with flap, are often used on a casual coat. Welt pockets, flap pockets are dressier. There are many variations.

Patch pocket

A patch pocket on a coat or suit must be lined. Cut the pocket from the coat fabric, and the lining piece from the coat lining. Make the lining 1/8 inch smaller than pattern.

Sew the right side of the lining to the right side of the pocket at the top edge. Leave 2 inches open in the center. Fold back on the hemline, with the right sides together. Stitch the edges on the seam allowance line. Trim seam and clip curve.

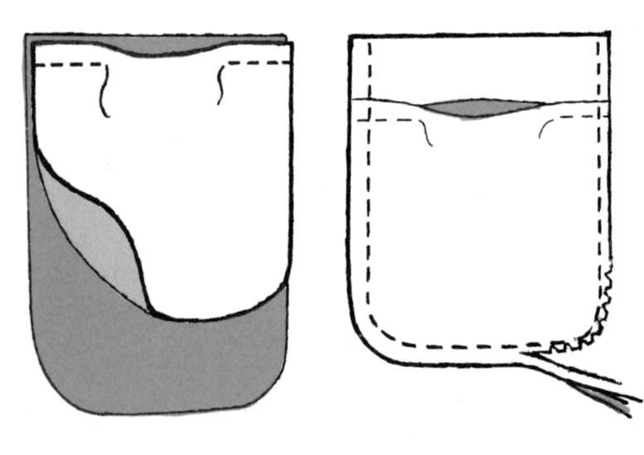

Turn the pocket right side out through the opening at the hem.

Slip-stitch the opening. Then baste around the pocket. The lining,

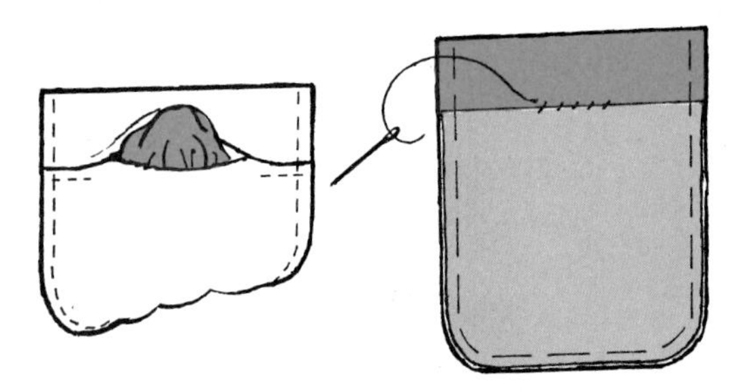

which was cut smaller, will be 1/8 inch in from the pocket edge.

Sew the pocket to the coat by hand or by machine. Top-stitch about 5/8 inch in from the pocket edge. Slip-stitch the edges by hand, or use a trim stitch all around the pocket before it's sewed by hand to the coat. Use a buttonhole twist.

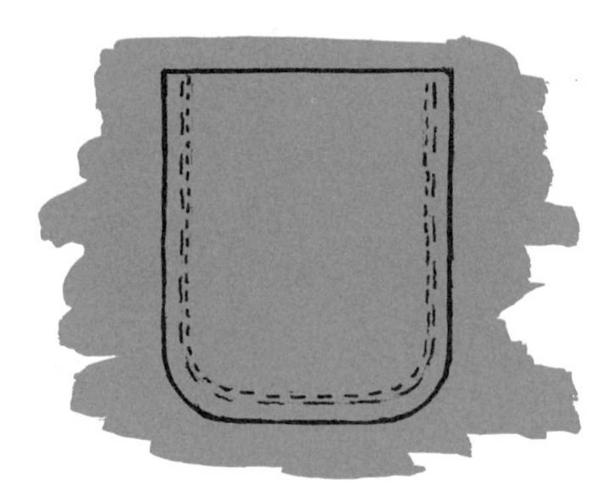

Pocket with flap

A flap is often used on a patch pocket. Line the flap with coat lining. If the fabric needs body, interface it. Stitch interfacing to outside seamline of the flap.

Trim 1/8 inch off the lining. Sew it to the flap, with right sides together and edges even. Trim seam and clip all around the curved edge.

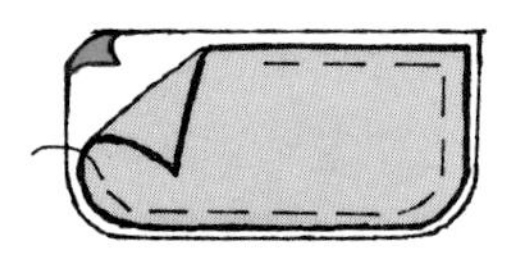

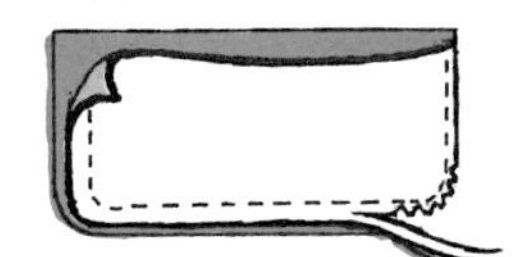

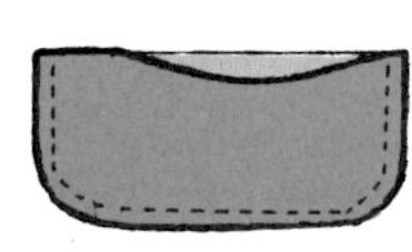

Now turn pocket flap right side out; then baste, and press edge.

Top-stitch 5/8 inch in from the finished edge of the flap.

Stitch the pocket flap 3/4 inch above the pocket, with right side of flap to coat. Trim seam to 1/4 inch.

Turn flap down over pocket and top-stitch 5/8 inch down from seam.

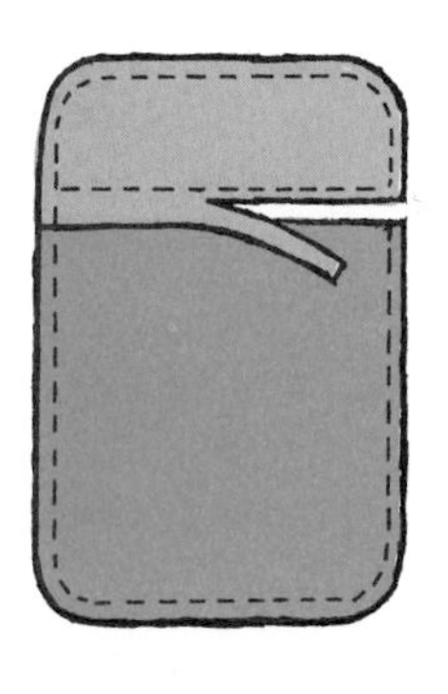

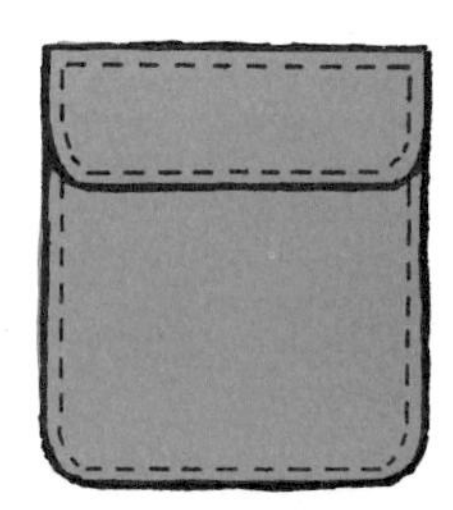

Inside flap pocket

Mark the position of the flap pocket on the coat with a basting thread. Use a strip of nonwoven interfacing under the coat, where the pocket will go. It gives body, and the pocket is easier to make.

Make the flap as for a patch pocket. Pin the raw edge of the flap to the top of the basting line, right side of flap to right side of coat. Stitch on the seam allowance line.

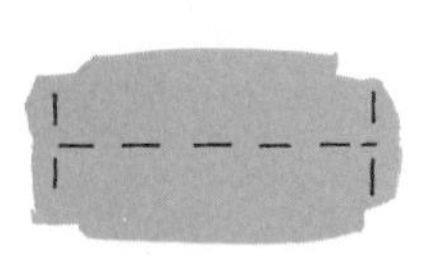

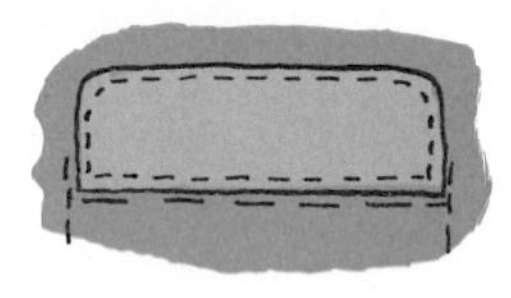

Cut pocket pieces from coat fabric. Make them 2½ inches deep, 2 inches wider than flap. Stitch one piece with the edge along the stitching line of the flap. Stitch on the seam allowance line, with stitches just clearing flap edge underneath.

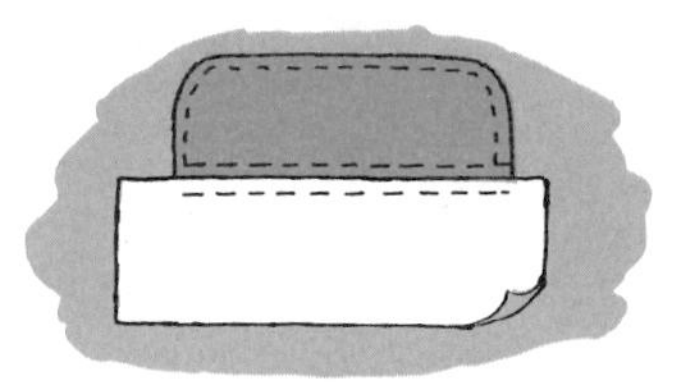

Turn to the wrong side. Slash between stitching lines to ½ inch of the ends. Clip diagonally to the corners. Turn the pocket piece to the wrong side. Fold a pleat at either end, forming a welt at the lower pocket opening. Then stitch into position from the right side.

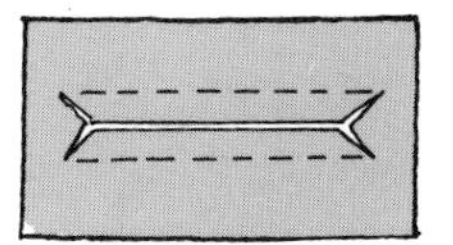

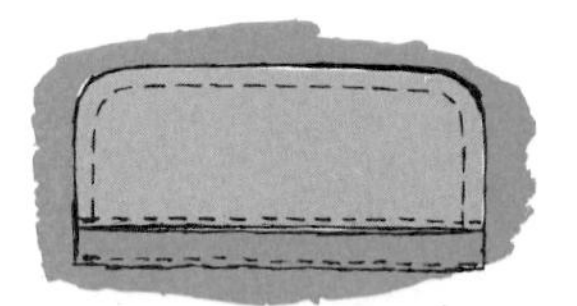

Turn the coat back. The small point at the end of the pocket is visible over the end of the welt. Stitch the point across this end. Flap turns down on the outside; the flap seam turns up on the inside. Sew the pocket piece (with lower lining added) along the welt seam. Sew around the

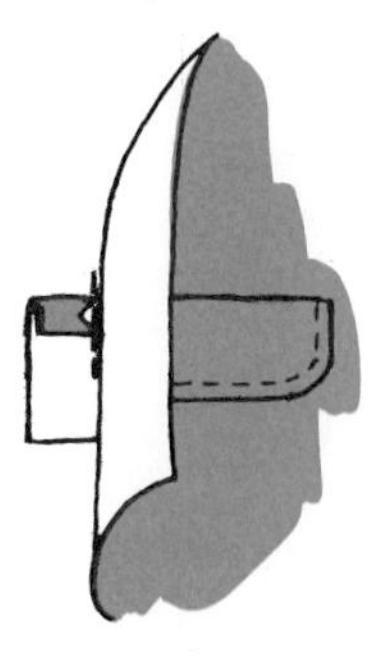

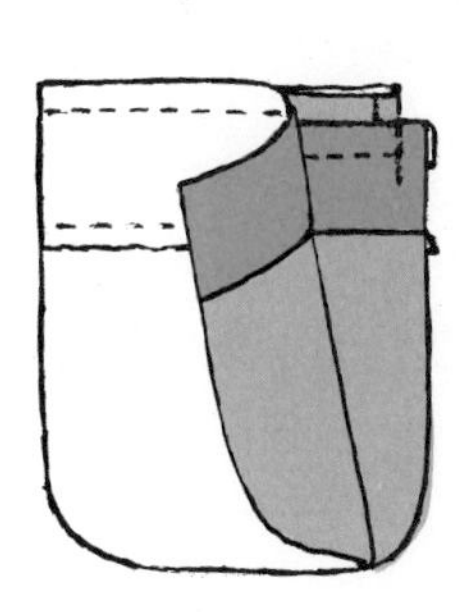

pocket pieces on the inside, and the coat pocket is finished.

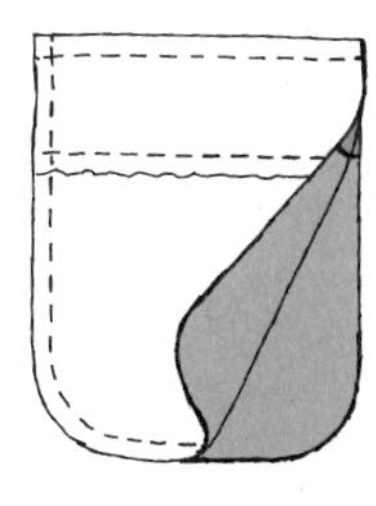

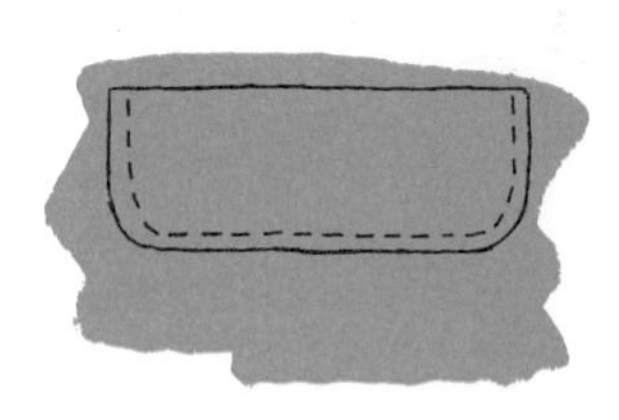

Simulated patch pocket

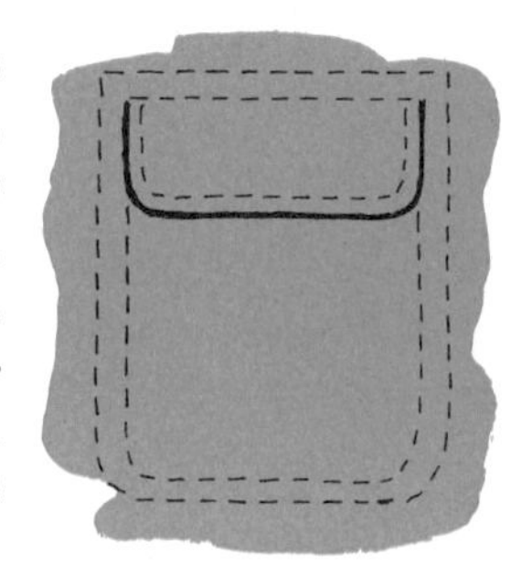

After you have finished pocket, turn the coat to right side. Run basting - stitch, outlining pocket, catching all the thicknesses together.

Stitch along this line by machine. Mark a second row $5/8$ inch from the first one and stitch by machine. This style resembles a patch pocket, but gives a more tailored look.

Diagonal welt pocket

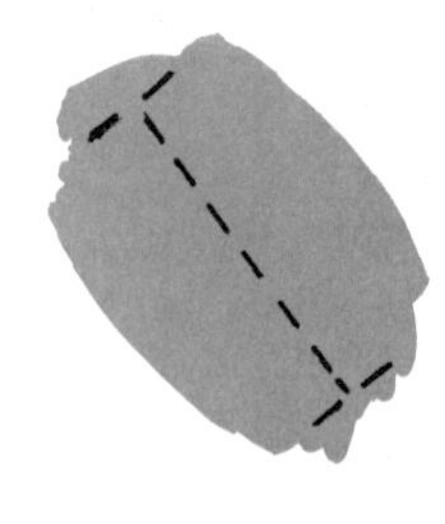

Mark the position for a welt pocket with basting line on right side of coat. Underline it with a nonwoven interlining. Cut two shaped welt pieces from coat fabric, one piece from interfacing. Sew interfacing to welt facing. Pin welt and facing, with right sides together, and stitch. Trim the seam and clip to the stitching line on the curved edges. Turn

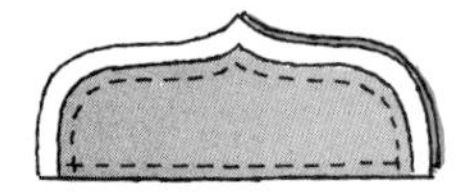

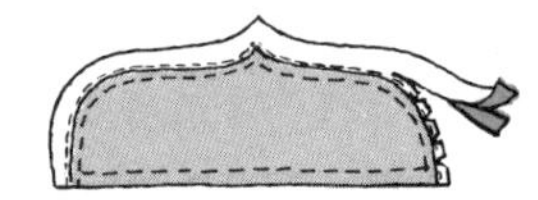

to the right side and baste in place. Press, and then stitch all around.

Interfacing is now available with an adherent that lets you press it to fabric with no sewing needed. The new interfacings are fine for welts, flaps, and other pocket detail.

Place the welt on the lower side of the pocket line of the coat and stitch on the seam allowance line. Pin the upper pocket piece on upper side of the pocket line, with the

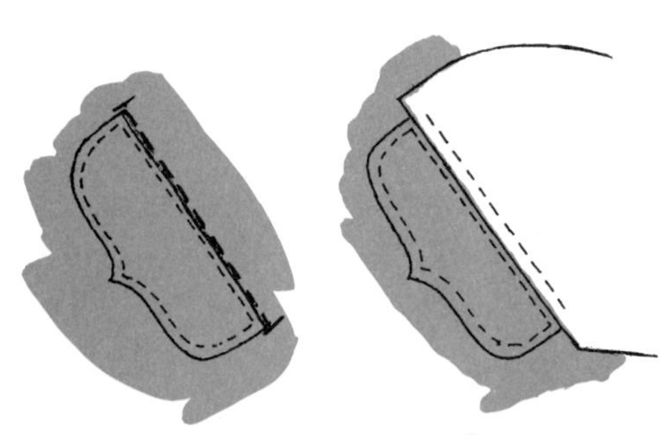

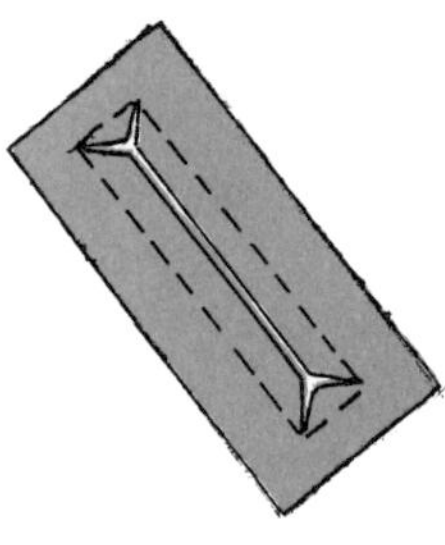

raw edge lapped to stitching line of welt. Stitch on the seam allowance line—which should just clear edges of welt underneath. Turn to inside. Slash between two rows of stitching to $1/2$ inch of either end. Slash diagonally into corners. Turn pocket piece to wrong side. Welt turns up on outside; seam allowance

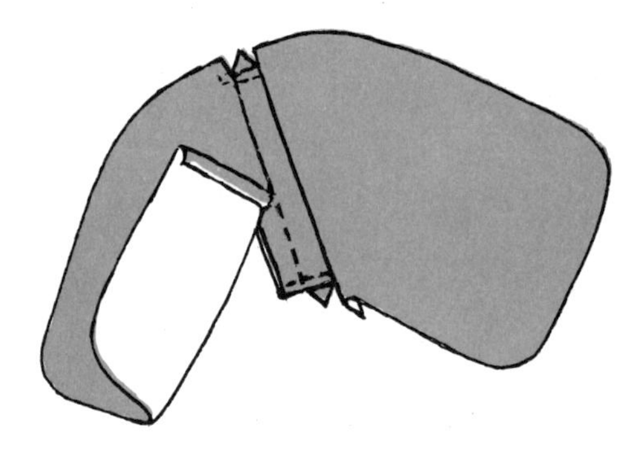

turns down on inside. Stitch under pocket to seam of welt on inside; sew

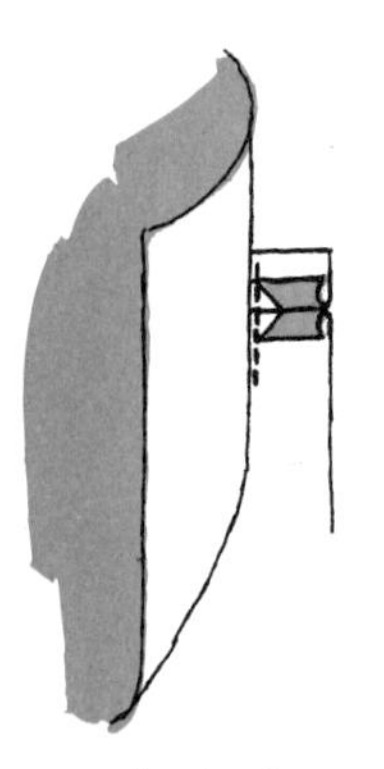

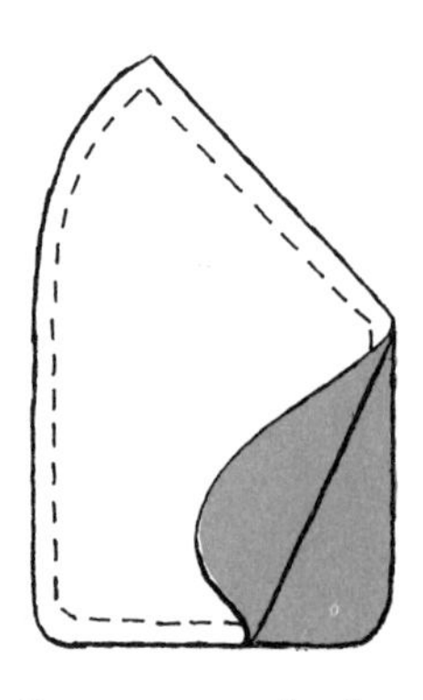

pocket pieces together around edges, catching points at corners. Turn to right side. Press welt up. Stitch around sides with a slip-stitch or on machine along trim stitch. Do same if welt is on straight of goods.

Seams

Plain seam

For general sewing, a plain inside seam is used on a coat. However, many interesting trim ideas can be worked out, using different types of seams. The coat doesn't have to be cut in any special way to take advantage of these interesting seams.

You can add trimming detail on the original seamlines of your coat.

Welt-seam Slot-seam

Slot-seam

Hand-baste or machine-baste the regular seam and press it open. On the wrong side of the seam, place a strip of fabric the length of the seam, but slightly wider than the seam allowances. Baste the center of it down the middle of the seam. On the right side, run two rows of basting an equal distance on either side of the center seam. Catch seam allowances underneath and strip of fabric all together in your basting. Stitch along these lines. Remove original basting stitch. Seam will spread, showing some underlay.

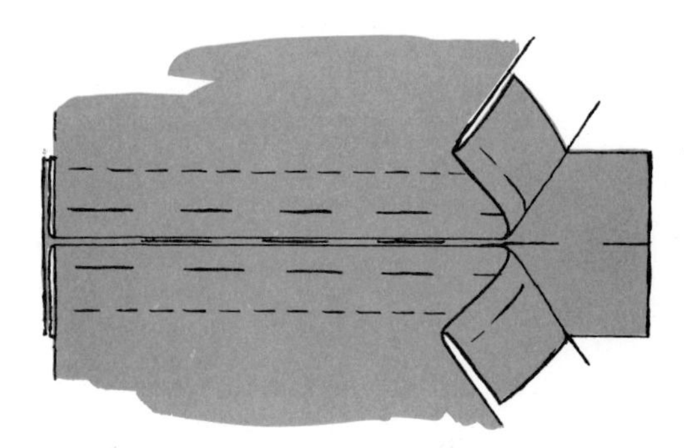

Welt-seam

This seam is suitable for extremely heavy fabrics. Sew up the seams, with right sides together. Decide which side of the seamline should have the welt. Cut the seam to ¼ inch on this side. Press the other seam over this trimmed edge and stitch. Distance you stitch from the seam will be the width of the welt. This seam gives a more tailored look to a coat. Use it around armholes, yokes, and along sleeve seams.

When stitching, be sure the tensions on your machine are not too tight, and that pressure of presser foot is not too heavy for the fabric.

If you want a wide welt seam, make the original seam allowance wider when you cut the coat.

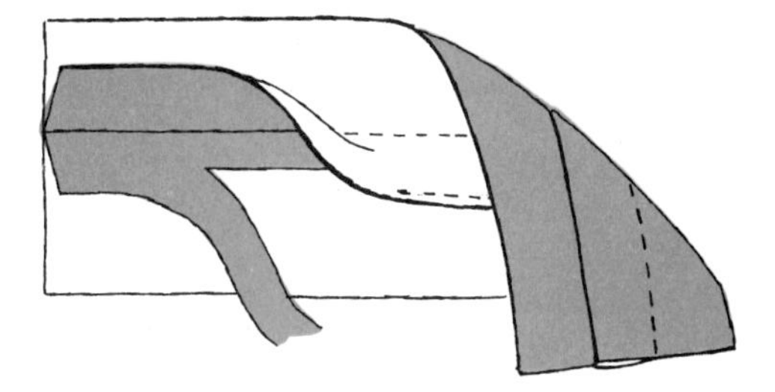

Tucked-seam

The seam allowances are generally

made wider when this seam is to be used. The tuck should have some width to be effective on a heavy coat.

Turn under the seam allowance on one edge and baste; lap this over the other edge so the raw edges meet at the inside. Stitch as far from folded edge as depth of tuck desired.

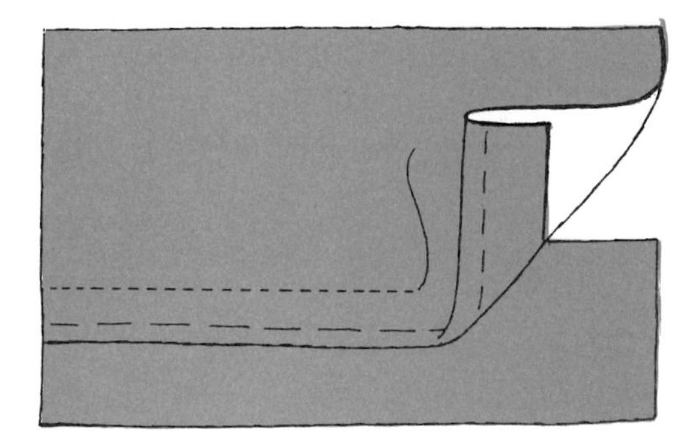

Double-welt seam

Make a welt seam. Turn to the right side and add another row of stitching close to the fold edge of seam.

This seam is frequently used on active sportswear, and it is often stitched in a contrasting color.

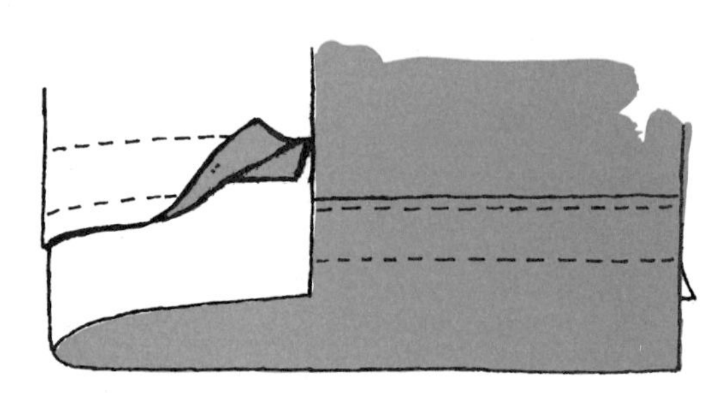

Bound-edge seam

Fold and press the seam binding so the under edge is slightly wider than upper edge. Press the seam open. If it has started to ravel, trim the edges. Slide the tape over the edge, with the narrow fold on top.

Stitch along the edge of binding, through three thicknesses of fabric. This seam is used on fabrics that ravel easily. It can also be used on jackets and coats that are unlined.

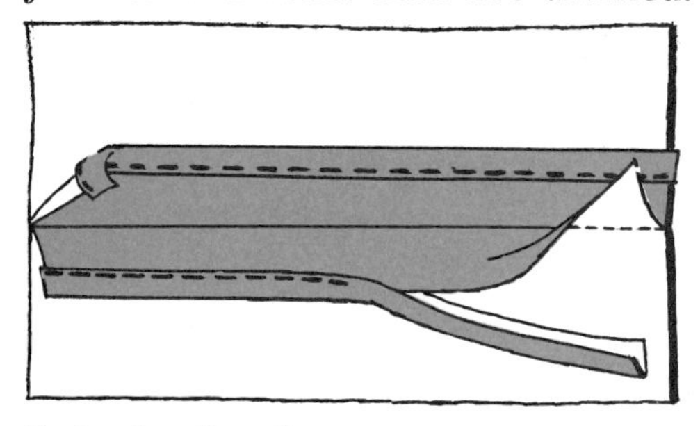

Stitched-edge seam

On lightweight fabrics, finish the edges by turning under 1/4 inch on each edge and stitching by machine. Stitch with loose tension close to the seam edge so that the seam won't pucker on the inside.

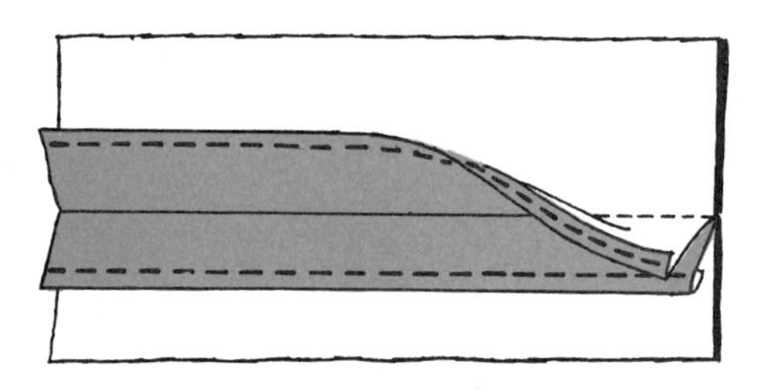

Hand-picking

This is done in matching buttonhole twist. Hold the garment with the right side toward you, and do a back-stitch. Take a small backstitch, slide the needle between the layers of fabric, and pick up a tiny stitch on wrong side. Bring needle to the right side again and take another back-stitch. When you come to the roll of your lapel, the underside of it is actually right side, so bring needle all the way through fabric. Do same back-stitch on the lapel side.

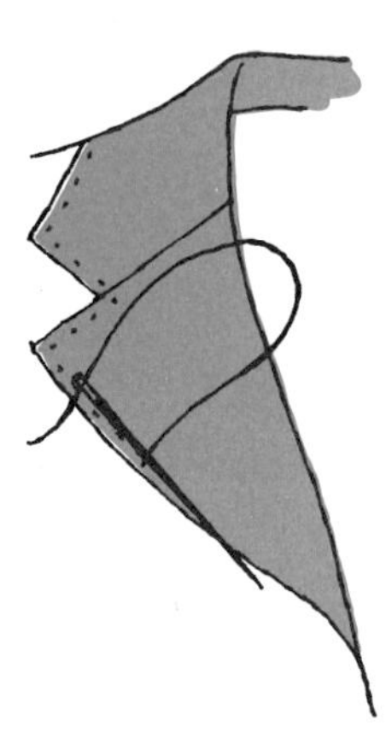

Lining coats and jackets

A fine lining in your coat gives it a tailored, professional look. A lining is usually of a much finer fabric than are the under fabrics. Linings are soft and firm, and are used to finish the inside of the garment. They also help to give body and texture, and add quality to the coat.

Lining a coat

Cut the lining from lining pattern. Mark and sew any darts or tucks in the lining. The back of lining has a pleat for ease. Press this pleat for the entire length. Sew by machine across the top, close to the neck to hold pleat in place.

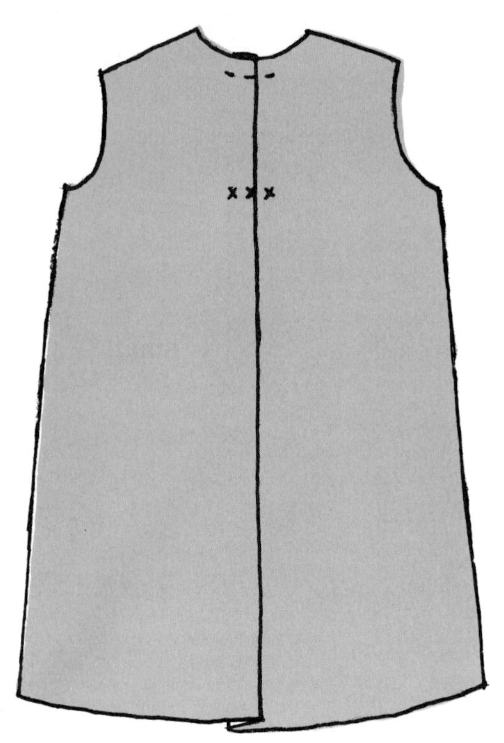

Sew up the side seams and shoulders. If the back neck has no facing, the back shoulder seam will be longer than the front, which is cut off to finish at the front facing. When the shoulders are stitched, leave ⅝ inch of the seam allowance open at the front shoulder. Press open all the seams of the lining. Lap the shoulder seam of the lining over the shoulder seam of the coat. Then tack the seams together.

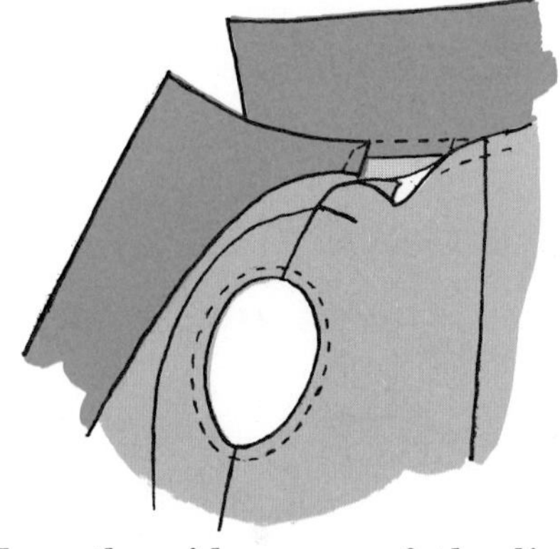

Lap the side seam of the lining over the side seam of the coat and pin to fit. Tack the seams together to about 6 inches from coat bottom.

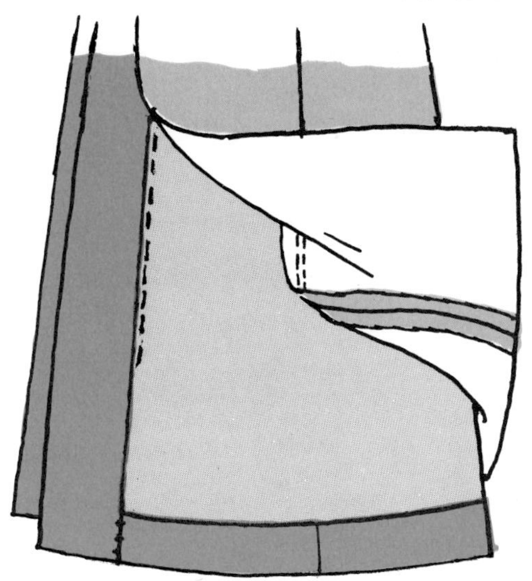

Clip to the seam allowance line all around the back neckline. Turn under a ⅝-inch seam, lap to the seam allowance at back neckline and pin.

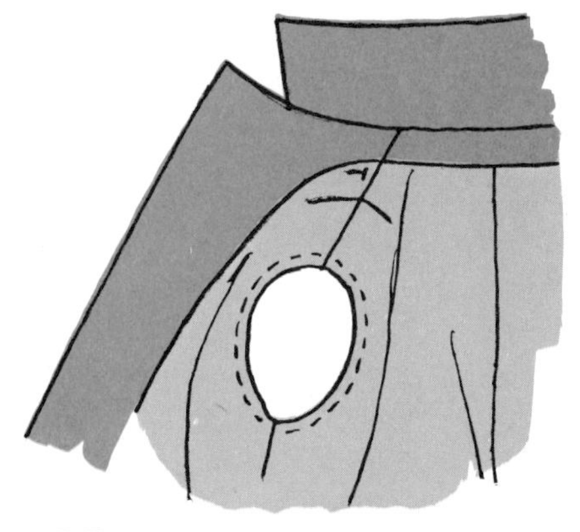

When pinning the front lining, start at the bottom of the coat. Measure at the side the amount the lining hangs below the coat. Check to see that the same amount extends below the coat in front. The reason for this is that the front lining is cut slightly on the bias along the bustline. By starting to pin the lining at the bottom and working up, the facing will be eased in over the bustline as it should be, and there

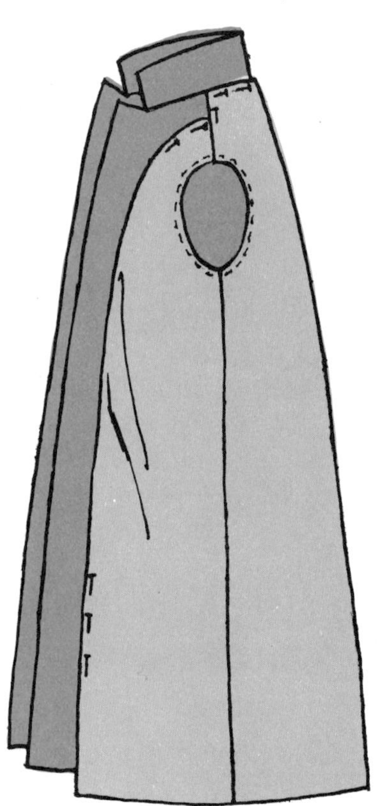

will be no possibility of the fabric stretching here, as often happens.

Turn under the seam allowance at the front and lap it over the front facing. Pin along both fronts. Slip-

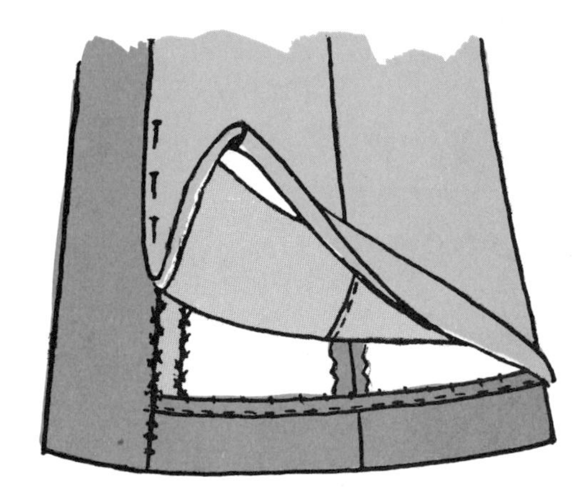

stitch the lining to the facing and back neck. Leave about 6 inches of the lining free at the lower end of the facing. The hem turns up over the interlining where it is sewed.

The lower edges of the lining can now be sewed to the facings.

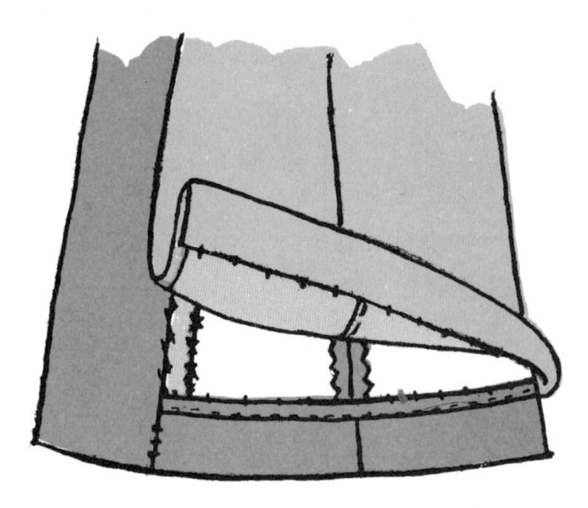

Baste lining to armhole seam. Sew up the sleeve lining. Turn the coat sleeve and sleeve lining inside out.

Place the wrong side of the sleeve lining against the wrong side of the coat sleeve. Lap lining seams over the coat seams. Tack the seams together by hand to about 3 inches above the sleeve hem and to 2 inches from the top. Turn the coat sleeve inside the lining of the sleeve.

To do this, put your hand in the lining and turn it over the sleeve.

Turn under the seam allowance at the top of sleeve. Lap it to the armhole seam allowance and pin the sleeve to fit.

Sew the sleeve lining by hand. Pin the lining to the sleeve about 5 inches above the hem. Then turn under the lining at lower edge of the sleeve and pin over the edge of hem. Slip-stitch it by hand. Lining folds down in the sleeve, making a shallow fold just below the stitching. This gives a little ease in the lining so that the sleeve will hang smoothly and not draw or pucker unattractively.

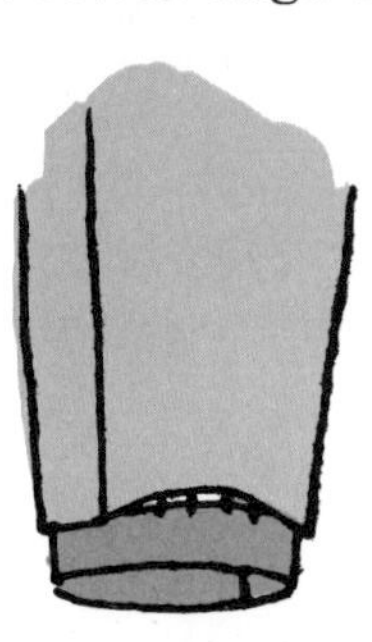

Use long French tacks to hold the

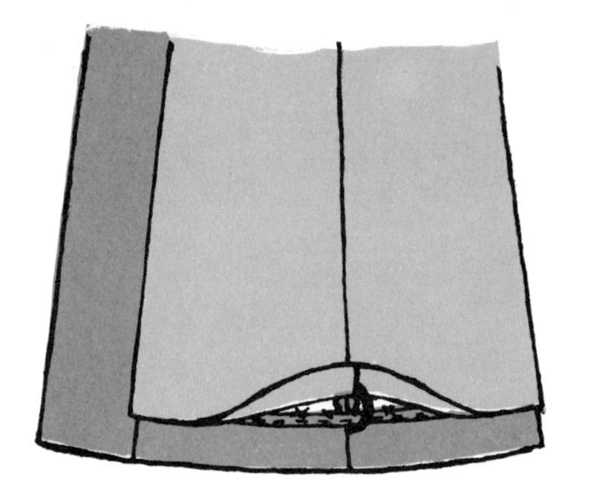

lining to the coat at the side seams at the hemline. Stitch holds lining firm, yet does not show.

Lining a jacket

Line the jacket the same as a coat, except at the lower edge. On a short jacket, the lining is attached at hemline. Trim the lining even with the finished jacket length.

Baste the lining to jacket about 5 inches above the hem. Turn under the seam allowance at the lower edge of the lining and lap over the raw edge of hem. Pin, slip-stitch.

The extra length of lining will form a fold above the hem of jacket. Press. This extra fold will give ease, prevent drawing or puckering. The

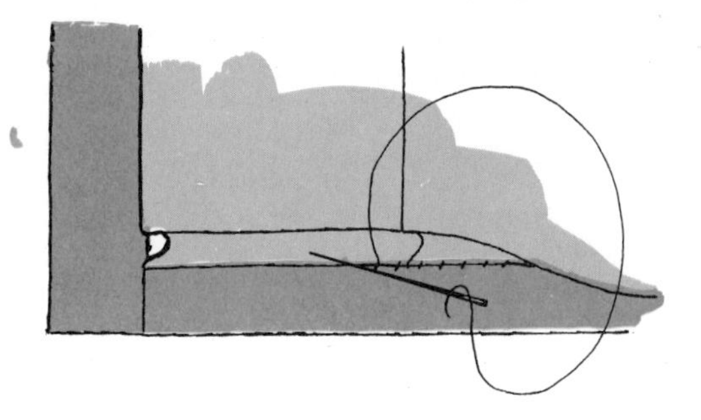

front lining, which was left unfinished to about 5 inches above the hem, can now be finished to the front facings of the jacket.

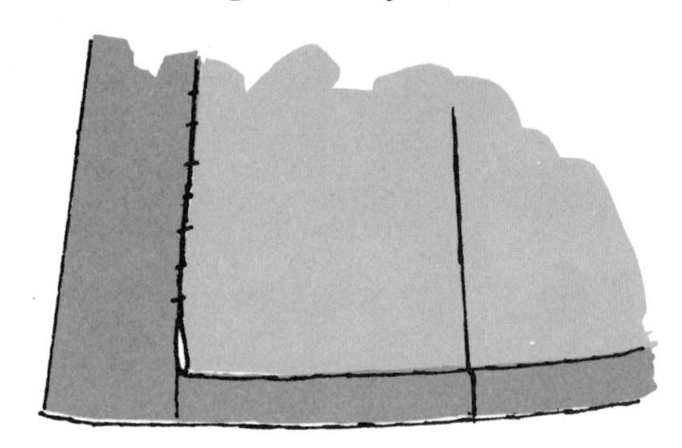

Linings can be made in contrasting colors or of a print to match a blouse or dress that you plan to wear under the coat or jacket.

Interlining

The interlining is a fabric used between the garment and the lining to give added warmth. It was formerly used only in coats, but since the advent of the winter suit, an interlining is also added to many suit jackets to give greater warmth.

There are two methods for applying the interlining. You can sew it to the lining before the lining is sewed together, much as if you were mounting the lining and interfacing. Or, it can be sewed directly to the coat or suit before the lining is put in.

Interlining fabrics

Lamb's wool makes the best interlining. You can buy it by the yard in piece goods departments. Lamb's wool is 54 inches wide, and is very soft and warm. There are also less expensive fabrics available for use as interlinings. Usually a store stocks several in a range of prices.

There are also linings available that have built-in warmth. Some have a soft interlining that's woven in on the wrong side of the lining itself. Others have a metallic backing that protects against heat or cold. These are easy to make up and sew.

Sewing lining and interlining together

In this method of interlining a coat, the lining and interlining are cut from the same pattern, except for the back. The back lining is cut with a pleat; the interlining is not. Press the back pleat in the lining. Place the wrong side of the back lining over the back interlining and sew all around.

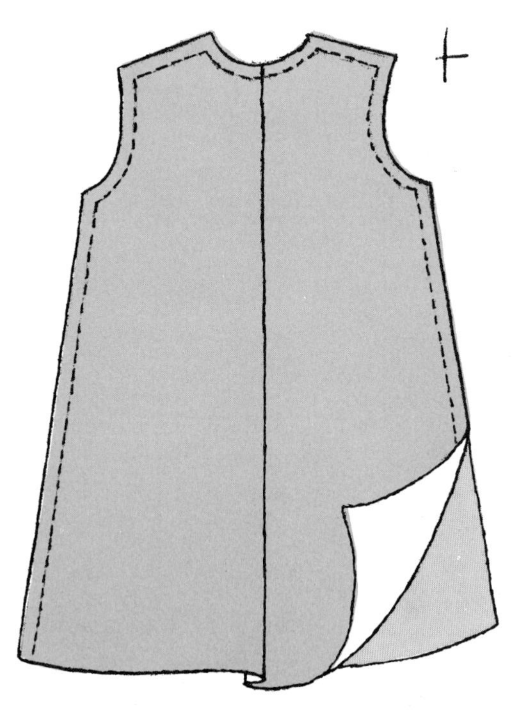

Sew the front lining pieces to the front interlining pieces. Then sew the darts or tucks in back and front

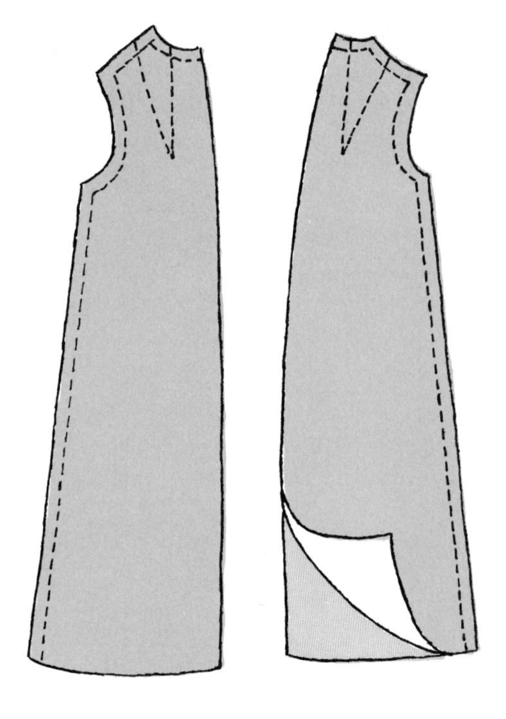

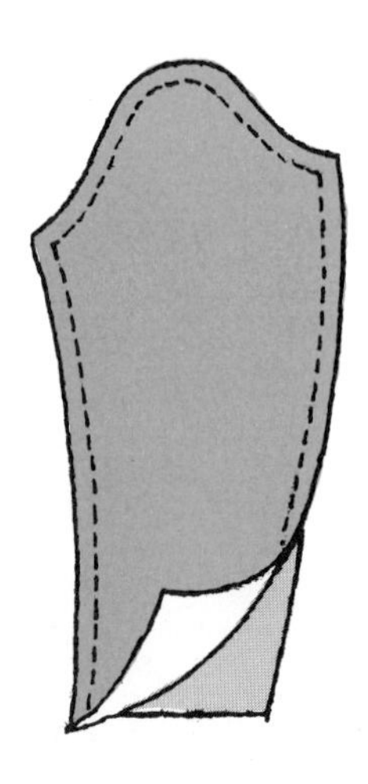

pieces. Sew up the side seams and shoulder seams of the coat lining.

Interline only the upper sleeve. Lining can then be fitted, sewed into the coat, as for a regular lining. See page 55 for information on regular lining.

Applying interlining directly to the coat

Cut the interlining from the lining pattern. Trim away the seam allowance down the front and around the back neckline. Cut the interlining away at the hem so it measures 1 inch shorter than the finished length.

Mark for the darts at the back and the front shoulders. Slash the darts and lap the amount the interlining is to be taken in, and top-stitch it so there is no bulk. This is the only machine-stitching you will have to do. Turn the coat inside out. Take the back interlining first and lap it over the side seam, the shoulder, and the back neck. Sew it by hand along

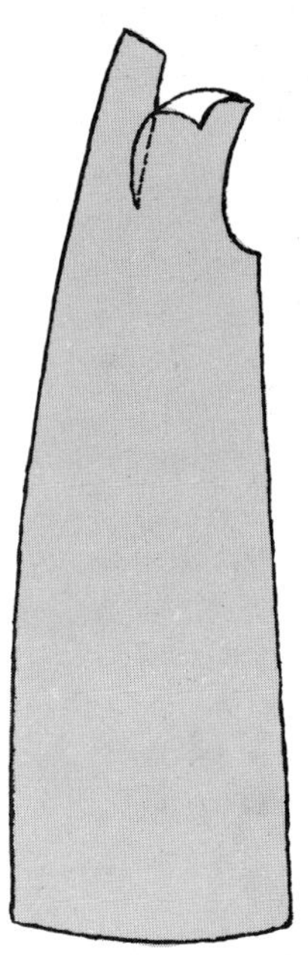

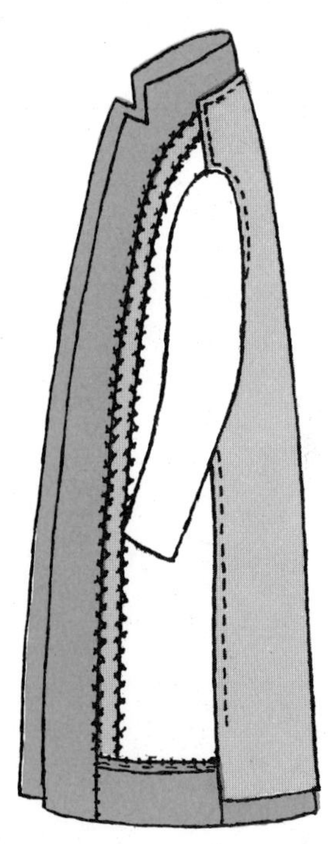

these seams. Next, apply the fronts. Lap front seams over the back at the

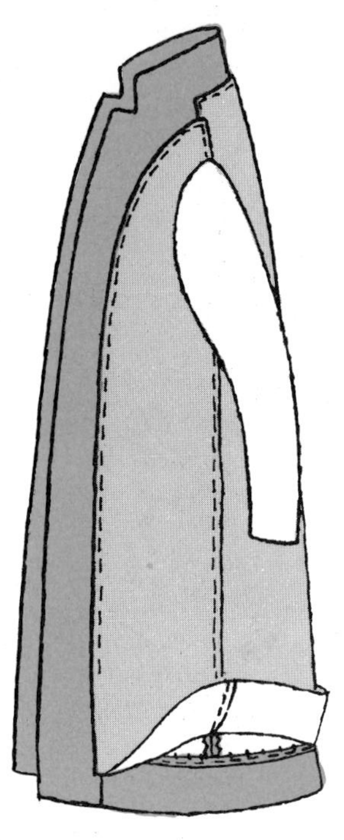

sides of the coat. Sew these in place with a loose running-stitch. Sew the interlining to the coat to within 6 inches of the hem. Below that, only back and front interlining seams are joined. Then lap the front shoulder seam over the back seam and tack.

The back interlining extends to the collar edge. In the front, it overlaps the facing edge for the entire length.

If the coat has a back neck facing, the back interlining will just lap this facing edge. Usually, only the upper

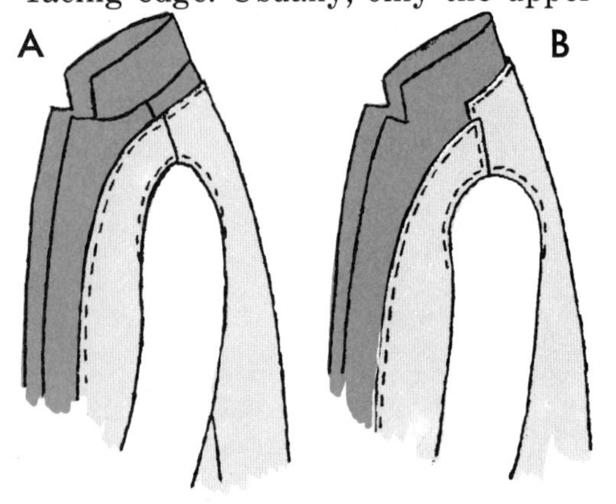

sleeve is interlined; however, if you need the added warmth, interline the under sleeve. It is sometimes advisable to interline the entire sleeve. Then you can also sew in an added panel by hand along the upper sleeve

for additional warmth in your coat.

Cut the interlining a little shorter than the finished sleeve length of the coat, so it just laps the hem edge. Next, carefully lap interlining along seam allowance line and tack. After

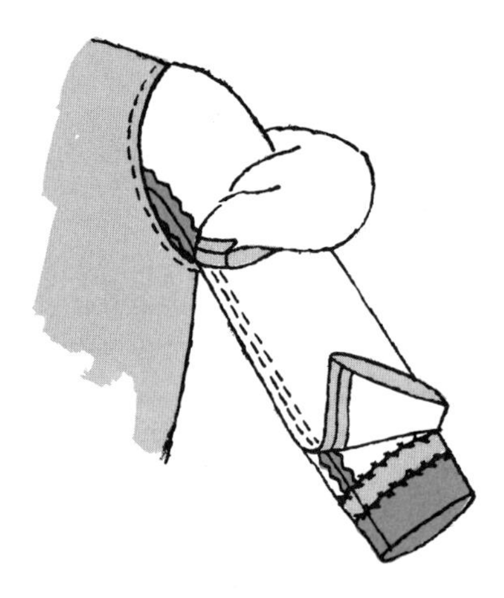

the interlining is attached, the lining can be fitted into the garment. Follow the instructions that are given on page 55 for lining a coat.

Adding warmth to interlining

Usually, the cold is felt across the back, over the chest, and at the outside of the arm. More warmth can be added at these points to equal the warmth that's offered by a fur coat.

Buy three large chamois skins; you can get them in hardware or auto supply stores. Cut and shape one to fit the back shoulders of the coat. Catch-stitch it to the interfacing only at the back. Split the second skin, cut and fit it to the front of the interlining over the chest. Catch-stitch this in place to the interlining. Then split and shape the third skin to fit the upper part of the sleeve. Catch-stitch this skin in place to the interlining only. This will add a great deal of warmth to a coat.

Fit the lining into the coat just as if the coat were not interlined.

Underlining suits and coats

Underlinings are even more important in tailoring than they are in dresses. It is sometimes necessary to use three or four different underlinings in one coat or suit to achieve the correct effect. Carefully analyze the pattern style, weight of fabric, and contour of the garment before choosing the underlinings and interfacings.

Don't confuse these two terms. The interfacing goes between the facing and front of the garment, and between upper and under collar. It serves an entirely different purpose than the underlining and must also be chosen with care.

Types of underlinings available

Each style must be carefully worked out, so the underlinings do the jobs they are best suited for. Except for hair canvas, the underlinings used for coats and suits are usually the special commercial ones. Tailored garments need a firmer underlining to support the heavier textures of suitings and coat fabrics. Also, commercial underlinings come in a wide range of finishes and weights, which is helpful in tailoring. Currently, there are approximately 18 woven underlinings and 12 nonwoven ones on the market for you to choose from.

Hair canvas has been used for years for tailoring collars and lapels and is also available in many weights and a few additional colors. There is a tissue-weight hair canvas that can be used for suits made in silk or sheer woolens. Hair canvas in this weight and slightly heavier ones can also be used as underlinings; an entire garment could be mounted on them.

Using underlining

First, check the garment fabric you have chosen. Whether it is a hard-finished worsted or suiting, a soft wool, or even tweed, the whole suit or coat should be mounted on an underlining. The crisper fabrics will take a soft woven underlining. These fabrics don't need more crispness, but only the added body that the underlining will give. An underlined suit or coat holds its shape better and needs less pressing. The hand finishing is inconspicuous because it is all sewed to the underlining, rather than to the upper fabric.

A crisp-finish, woven underlining would be the best choice to give added body and firmness to a soft wool or tweed upper fabric.

Regardless of the upper fabric, use a hair canvas or a woven interfacing for a notched collar and lapel. To make it correctly, it must be shaped and molded. (See page 21.)

When a coat or suit has a definite contour, or shaping that is vital to the style, the underlining should be firm enough to hold the contour. Use nonwoven in the heavier weight, or a woven underlining with a very crisp finish. The front of the coat or jacket can be faced with hair canvas or any woven or nonwoven interfacing.

When there is no lapel to be rolled, a woven underlining is not essential. A Peter Pan style collar is best made with a hair canvas interfacing.

Pocket flaps can be made with nonwoven underlining with adherent. You may use several underlinings in one coat for the proper effects.

INDEX

A-B

C

D-F

H-I

J-L

N-P

R-S

T-U-W